THE **OFFICE** THAT **GROWS**
YOUR BUSINESS

Achieving Operational Excellence in Your Business Processes

Written by the Faculty and Staff of the Institute for Operational Excellence

Foreword by Kevin J. Duggan

Copyright © 2009 by The Institute for Operational Excellence.

All rights reserved. No part of this book may be reproduced or utilized in any form or by any means, electronic or mechanical, including photocopying, recording, or by any information storage and retrieval system, without permission in writing from the publisher.

Cover design contributors: Kevin Sawyer, Janine Calise, Peter Burgess, and Lisa Burgess.

Printed and manufactured in the United States of America.

Library of Congress Control Number 2009937795

ISBN 978-0-9841843-0-9

Contents

Acknowledgements iii

Foreword v

Prologue 1

Chapter 1: The Hornet's Nest 3

Chapter 2: The Investigation 11

Chapter 3: The Game Plan 22

Chapter 4: The Old Friend 29

Chapter 5: The Fateful Day 39

Chapter 6: The Education, Part I 52

Chapter 7: The Education, Part II 76

Chapter 8: The Tour 93

Chapter 9: Sharing the Knowledge 108

Acknowledgements

While many people at The Institute for Operational Excellence contributed their time and efforts developing the concepts and writing for this book, the project team spent many long hours creating and refining this material. The Institute would like to recognize and thank Jim Kemp, James Marrese, Kevin Duggan, Gene Burk, and Kirk Bolton for making this book possible.

Many other people supported the project team in their endeavors. The Institute would like to recognize and thank Elizabeth Duggan, Jennifer Krider, Susan Carroll, and Bridget Snow for their hard work and tireless dedication.

Foreword

Operational Excellence. Corporate leaders embrace it for a competitive edge in today's challenging global market. It's heralded as the antidote to slipping revenues. And industry titans like Toyota tout it as a business necessity[1]. But what exactly is it?

While more and more companies are aggressively pursuing Operational Excellence by employing six sigma, lean, and other continuous improvement methods, the concept itself remains vague. It has yet to be practically defined in a way that can be taught and applied, especially to industries other than manufacturing. The result: companies comprised of mostly offices and business processes, such as insurers, hospital administrative practices, financial companies, banks, and service organizations, lack an applicable definition of Operational Excellence. And there is little – if any – written material on how to achieve it in the office. Until now.

To achieve Operational Excellence, you need more than just a strong leader with passion and drive. The key ingredient is practical knowledge that can be applied quickly and easily by following a process, a step-by-step guide to move from point A to point B. Like a roadmap, the process can be read, taught, and shared with each employee to rapidly move a company forward.

That process is described in the pages that follow. The knowledge is practical and hands-on, but told through a story to make it more realistic.

---

[1] Liker, Jeffery K. The Toyota Way: 14 Management Principles From The World's Greatest Manufacturer. McGraw-Hill. New York, New York, 2004.

It's not intended to solve a problem or provide a solution. In fact, this type of thinking is what often restricts companies from achieving Operational Excellence. Rather, the information provided explores different concepts and ways of thinking to offer a fresh look at the office and business processes. It's intended to educate and teach companies *how to grow their business by achieving Operational Excellence in their offices.*

I hope you enjoy the Institute's first book in a series on achieving Operational Excellence. Each one provides a detailed, practical approach that enables a unique area of the business to achieve Operational Excellence quickly. Once applied to all areas of the organization, the end result is a business that does not need to rely on hiring the right person, strong leadership, or innovative products to grow. It's *a business that is designed to grow year after year.*

Enjoy reading, apply the knowledge, and grow your business!

Kevin J. Duggan

Founder, Institute for Operational Excellence

Prologue

I remember the day that changed my professional life forever. The day I learned things that altered my view of continuous improvement. The day I saw a business that had harnessed its efforts to not only get better each day, but to improve business growth and performance. The day I learned that a company that achieves Operational Excellence is much more than an organization that does things efficiently and waste free: it's a company that has developed and applied fundamental principles for sustained business growth. It was quite a day.

On that day, I heard Operational Excellence defined in a way that was easy to understand, applicable at all levels of an organization, and effective at aligning everyone toward a common destination. I also had the privilege of seeing the definition come to life when I walked through an office and saw Operational Excellence in action.

Don't get me wrong – I'm not a newcomer to all of this. I was previously well read in continuous improvement and was striving to create a culture of continuous improvement at my company. I had used my knowledge of lean, six sigma, and the successful Toyota production system to make some improvements in my company's business processes recently, and thought I knew how to effectively use the latest tools and techniques.

But, I was wrong. Dead wrong. Sure, the tools worked. And by applying them, I was making progress. However, looking back, I was improving about as fast as a turtle crossing the highway. The journey seemed endless, with no destination in sight. I realized on that fateful day that anything we do to try to improve our business processes in the office must be geared toward supporting business growth. It not only has to drive bottom line results. It has to lay a foundation or provide a structure from which we can grow our business.

As if that wasn't enough of a game-changer, I was shocked to learn that companies achieve Operational Excellence *in months*, not years. And it doesn't require a strong leader to drive the change and sustain it. It takes education, and boy did I get some. I discovered that Operational Excellence is not a vague or ambiguous place, but rather a tangible destination that can be achieved by following a roadmap. Most importantly, because it's achieved through a process, it can be taught, which means the knowledge can be shared and applied quickly throughout the entire organization.

Even though I didn't get all the details when I learned about Operational Excellence for the first time, the knowledge was simple and intuitive. I understood enough to be able to go back and begin educating people in my own office about the concepts, including my boss.

To think that there was a time when I had never heard of takt capability, work-flow cycles, guaranteed turnaround times, single point initialization, standard work at the flow level, and *an office that operates without management*. But I'm getting ahead of myself. The real story begins a few days earlier, when I returned from a week-long conference. While I was gone, something had gone seriously wrong back at my office…

The Hornet's Nest

It was Monday morning, but I was anxious to get to work after a week at a conference full of insurance adjusters, most of them excited about recent changes to the Medicare/Medicaid verbiage. It's a topic we have to untangle for our business plans, but I was admittedly distant, more curious to see how my team was doing back at the office in my absence. The last few weeks had been hectic, but everyone seemed to pull together with some very creative solutions. I left the office confident in how my team would perform while I was away. Confirming my expectations, I didn't get any calls during the conference – a good, albeit unusual, sign.

At the conference registration, I bumped into Peyton Peterson, a classmate from my undergraduate days. I had lost track of Peyton over the years, but at these massive conferences, I'd learned the hard way that it's generally best to share a table with someone you know versus a stranger who may have peculiar habits. Recalling Peyton's studious characteristics and common sense, I asked, "Want to share a table at the conference?"

Peyton's reply surprised me. "Sure, maybe we can catch up on things during break. But I really want to learn this material."

Good choice, Pat, I thought. "No distractions here," I said.

Over the course of the week, I learned that Peyton faced the same career dilemma I had a year earlier, so I offered some counsel – at breaks, of course.

I explained to Peyton that I had been working in the accounts receivable department at a local 500-bed hospital. "The job was secure, the hospital was solvent, and I had moved up from a college intern spot to a full-time position. I had overcome my earlier identity as an intern and convinced management that I was ready for a supervisory role."

"How did you accomplish that?" asked Peyton. "I'm still suffering a bit from the intern image and would like to understand what you did to get them to recognize your abilities. My goal is to become the divisional expert on this Medicare/Medicaid topic we're learning about this week."

I told Peyton my brief work history. "Some of it was luck, but mostly it was lemonade from lemons. Over a few years, I had made numerous lateral moves that exposed me to many areas of the business and several departmental managers. I observed and analyzed different management styles and chose to emulate those that worked best as I worked on my own future. I felt pretty fortunate to have had those opportunities, not to mention all the technical knowledge I gained from bouncing around between different areas of the business."

"I see how the lemonade strategy worked for you," said Peyton. "But I'm on my second manager now, studying lean tools, and I don't exactly get the feeling that I'm on the fast track. I think it's going to take something else."

"I was lucky…sort of," I explained. "My employees performed well, met and exceeded the goals set for them, and made me a valuable asset to the company in the process. I thought that was going to be my ticket to bigger and better things, but I soon learned that being a valued supervisor wasn't necessarily the best thing for my career. It was clear that I had become so good at what I was doing that I was never going to get promoted.

"Maybe I should have discussed my situation with my manager or someone who could have given me advice. But, as they say, timing is everything. I took a phone call from a recruiter and entertained an inquiry from an insurance company. Even though I didn't know anything about claims processing, I was a lifetime learner and a good supervisor, and knew I was ready to get my feet wet as a department manager."

"So, you didn't get into management by becoming a technical expert?" asked Peyton.

"Well, yes and no," I said. "Initially, I became technically savvy to demonstrate competence to my superiors. Then, I started looking at the bigger picture and where I wanted to be in three to five years. The fastest way to get somewhere is to know where your journey will take you. Keep that in mind as you strive for that expert status you mentioned. You might be valuable, but you might be *too* valuable to be promoted."

I wondered if I was still trying to justify my decision to leave the hospital. Things had been comfortable there, and steady. Insurance, on the other hand, is about risk, in more ways than one, and the past eight months at my new job had not always been comfortable.

The insurance claims business was new to me when I started. With my prior experience in hospital accounts receivable, I had dealt with the insurance market for years and learned that some claims processors were much more capable than others. My reputation was equally known. One of the less respected but larger insurance companies had gotten to know me better than either of us would have liked because of constant expedites, quality problems, and settlement errors. They had some chronic issues they genuinely wanted to fix, but they continued to be unsuccessful. When the recruiter contacted me, she explained the situation, their challenges, and their commitment to fixing this problem by hiring a professional from the outside.

I was initially intrigued, but she really got my attention when she told me they wanted to hire a manager that could apply lean teachings. It was an exciting challenge to start fresh at a company and have the chance to fix some of their problems.

A cheery voice from the ordering window at my local coffee house interrupted my reflections. "Good morning, Pat. Your usual?"

"Yes, grande latte, two shots of espresso. Thanks." Moments later, I took my coffee and drove toward the office, sipping while trying to avoid the potholes and the few other drivers on the road.

When I got to work, I easily found a good parking spot in the lot, grabbed my briefcase, and cradled that precious coffee as I stepped out of my car. Soon, I was walking briskly toward the seven-story building and planning out my day in my head. I'd come in early to try to make a dent in the backlog that had accumulated while I was at the conference. At this hour, there would be no people, and no people meant no distractions.

When I was almost within the shadow of the building, it happened. The lights came on in my boss's corner office on the third floor. It's okay, I thought. I'll just quietly enter my office. I can still get an hour to myself to wade through all the emails, voicemails, and memos that are no doubt waiting for me. After that, when the workday officially starts, I'll have finished my coffee and can check in with Chris.

I'll take the stairs rather than the elevator, I thought, as I made my way through the lobby. It'll be a bit more clumsy with this coffee, but I can control the staircase door and close it quietly to get in unnoticed. There's no need to disturb the boss, who probably wants to get on top of the chaos before a fresh round hits us this week. This way, we'll both be able to get a good, uninterrupted start.

I made it into my office without any loud noises: no doors slamming, no laptops crashing onto desks, no chairs banging into walls. Generally, Chris sings out a greeting when it becomes apparent I've arrived, and the absence of a welcome suggested I might have some solitude.

I carefully set the coffee on my desk and started to organize the mess. A healthy dose of voicemails, emails, and post-it notes. Where to begin? Post-it notes are urgent because they were delivered in person. Voicemail is next because someone couldn't wait for a conventional response. Email is next, and then the in-basket.

I pulled the post-it notes off my desk like I was an archeologist doing a forensic analysis at a dig site. Obviously, the ones on top were the most recent, but perhaps had a linkage to some of the ones buried deeper. I reviewed them one by one, matched them with their predecessors, and then arranged the piles into two groups: action items and status reports. There was only one action item, and that could wait until everyone else arrived.

Next was the voicemail. I reached for the phone and it rang as I touched the handset. Startled, I jumped and almost spilled my coffee all over my desk. I caught my breath and grabbed the receiver before the second ring, thinking I might be able to prolong my solitude if Chris hadn't heard it. Answer quietly, I thought.

"Good morning, this is Pat," I said in a strong but quiet tone. "How can I help you?" Unfortunately, I didn't have the presence of mind to check the caller ID before I picked up the phone.

"Ah ha! I sensed you were here, and I saw your office light spilling into the hallway," said Chris. "But I expected you to stop by as usual. Have you checked your email yet?"

"No," I replied, "I was just getting to my voicemail when you called. What can I do for you?"

"So you haven't gotten to your email yet?" repeated Chris. "Then you don't know that Mercy Hospital, one of our biggest customers, is irate? I'm surprised no one contacted you while you were gone. Well, I'm glad you're here early. Come into my office. You don't need to go through all the email strings now. I'll fill you in on what's important, but you'll probably want to read through everything later tonight."

Later tonight? What does that mean? What had happened? During my eight months here, Chris had never been that direct. Whatever this is about, it must be serious – and might signal the end of the new-associate honeymoon. I grabbed my notepad and hurried into Chris's office.

"What's the situation?" I asked.

"Last week, we let a very important claim drop through the cracks, and it was late getting out to Mercy Hospital, one of our biggest customers. We were missing simple information on the claim, it got sidelined, and we didn't even notice it was late. Wednesday morning, the day it was targeted to clear, Mercy called us to get the status since it was a significant claim for them. When we had to request the missing information, it was obvious that we were just starting the claim. Worse, they said they'd charted a downward trend in our performance. They actually *anticipated* the claim would be late based on the poor performance record we'd generated over the past quarter and, since this claim was particularly large, they put us on watch.

"I had to get involved and was told by your team that for the past eight weeks, they'd been limiting the number of expedited claims allowed at any time to two, and they had already hit their max when the Mercy one rolled around. They were quick to explain that this system was effective in eliminating the daily peaks and valleys in their workload, and had allowed them to be more productive with fewer priority shifts."

At least my team understood the new system, could explain it, and were disciplined to the point of defending it, I thought. But my mind was racing, thoughts bouncing around like billiard balls off the break. What had gone wrong? We'd all agreed to the changes during a kaizen, or rapid improvement event. We tested the rules for six weeks and made adjustments as needed. We never had a challenge to the "two per day" limit during the whole trial period.

I wanted to speak, but Chris wasn't even taking a breath! "I then persuaded, no, I *told* them to expedite the Mercy Hospital claim, and Bob said he would shepherd it through. This was last Wednesday."

We didn't count on a claim being sidelined that long. But what does Chris want me to do? Change our standard operating procedure to make sure we always take care of Mercy Hospital first? Our intention was to treat all expedited claims the same, regardless of the customer. Chris knows this! We spoke about the issue at length.

"What's the status now?" I asked. "Did we get the check cut on Wednesday?"

"It finished on Friday at noon, two days later than they expected it," said Chris. "Your team offered reasons why it took so long. But I know this process. I worked my way up to this corner office by performing every task. And it shouldn't have taken that long to expedite – expedite! – a claim. There's no reasonable explanation for why we missed the target for that claim, just excuses! You know time is money, especially in this economy, and we cost Mercy two extra days.

"But that's not even the real issue. What's more concerning is that one of our customers seemed to know more about our performance than we did. So I had the IT department create a report for the last quarter showing how long each claim took to process, plus actual versus planned completion dates. I confirmed the downward trend, not only for Mercy Hospital, but for most of the claims we process. It creates a hefty cash float, which is positive for us, but bad for our customers. Based on our performance over the last quarter and what Mercy Hospital told me, we could be in danger of driving them to another partner! And, for all we know, other customers are thinking the same thing and just not telling us. Do you realize the financial hit we would take if that happened?"

Yes, I do, I thought. That's one of the things I came here to fix.

"Pat, I could ask you a number of questions right now, but I don't think you'd have answers for any of them. I realize you didn't gain your experience processing claims here like I did, but that doesn't matter now. We need results, and we need to come up with a corrective action plan very soon that demonstrates how committed we are to improving our performance for all of our customers. We can't just create a Mercy Hospital group and use it to expedite their claims. That won't get to the heart of the issue. We need to get better for everyone, Pat, or we'll lose them all.

"We need a corrective action plan, and it's your department's responsibility. I want to have that plan in my hands for review Tuesday afternoon, one that applies to Mercy Hospital *and* every other customer."

Chris paused for a second, then leaned in to give me some more personal guidance. "Look, Pat, you've only been here for eight months, and already I've seen some improvements. But we, and you, have a lot riding on this. I'm really troubled about the expedite criteria and the limit your team told me about. How can we serve our customers when we're only allowed to process two expedited claims at any given time? You can't control when something has to be expedited, Pat, you have to react to it. That's what good managers do. I don't think you can limit the number of expedited claims, Pat. That's where I'd start to look."

"Okay, Chris, I won't let you down," I said. "Things have been getting better over the past two months, at least from where I sit. I understand business, so I recognize our customers' cash flow is important. I'll start pulling some strategy together now and gather the team when they get in. I'll get right on this, and I'll check in with you later today to let you know where I'm headed."

"Okay," said Chris. "But remember, it isn't just me you have to satisfy, it's our entire customer base. We can't lose Mercy Hospital, or any other account. We brought you in here eight months ago to fix things, and much of our reasoning was based on how relentless you were in managing our account. I expect your doggedness to continue here. I know most of the associates in your department have other duties besides claims processing. They always have and always will. But this tardiness can't continue. Let me know if…"

"Thanks, Chris," I said. "I'm on it."

The Investigation

My mind was racing as I stepped out of Chris's office. I need to get my team together, go over what happened, get everyone on the same page, and then talk to them about the problems they're having with the new improvements we implemented. Once I do that, I'll come up with some solutions that apply to our major customers, sell the plan to Chris, and then begin implementing it immediately.

I heard the elevator doors open on my floor, but Bob was the only one who got off. I quickly approached him in the elevator alcove. I wanted to learn the details Chris didn't know. Bob has been here for years, and knows all the processes. He has become the answer man for everything but, unlike me, seems to be content with his status and has no desire to get into management.

"Bob, I'm glad you're here early," I said as he got off the elevator. "Chris informed me that Mercy Hospital is *irate*. I need to know what went wrong."

Bob stared at me, dumbfounded. A glazed look came over his eyes, like he'd had to tell this tale many times before. "So, Chris told you what happened?" he offered.

"Well, I was briefed on the high points," I said, "and given the assignment of developing a corrective action plan. But I really don't know the details. Can you fill me in?"

"Sure," he said, regaining some of his composure. "I figured you'd be here now, so I came in early, too. Here's the story, as I recall it. The Mercy Hospital claim started on time, but was missing some information. It was sidelined so we could obtain the info, but when the hospital called to inquire about the delivery, no one could find the file. After turning the department upside down, we eventually found it, still incomplete. We had to expedite the claim, even though it didn't fit our criteria and we had already reached our limit for the day. We got it out on Friday at noon.

"I didn't call you because when Chris said, 'Bob, expedite this claim, *now*, and I don't care about the criteria!' I had little doubt about what I should do. At that point, it was just a matter of doing it. Whether you knew or not wouldn't have changed things, so I decided to leave you alone at the conference."

"Okay, thanks for filling me in," I said. "As for Mercy, I'm not sure what to do right now. But the bigger issue is figuring out how to reverse a downward trend in timeliness, not just for Mercy, but for all our accounts."

I wondered what I would have done if I had been around when everything happened. Would I have overridden the procedures? Would that have been the right answer? Or would it have just opened the floodgates?

I collected myself and turned my attention back to Bob. "Here's what we're going to do," I said. "I want to get the team together and review how a claim is processed. I know it, and you know it, but I'm not sure everyone else understands what happens. Get everyone in the conference room when they come in and we'll go through the steps. Then, I want to hear all the problems they're having so I can figure out a solution."

Bob turned and hurried away. Okay, I'd better get a handle on this before everyone gets here. There isn't much time. I've only got a few minutes to frame the objective, scope, and strategy for the meeting. I'll review the departmental organizational chart, make copies, and bring them with me so everyone can see where everyone else fits in.

The Office That Grows Your Business

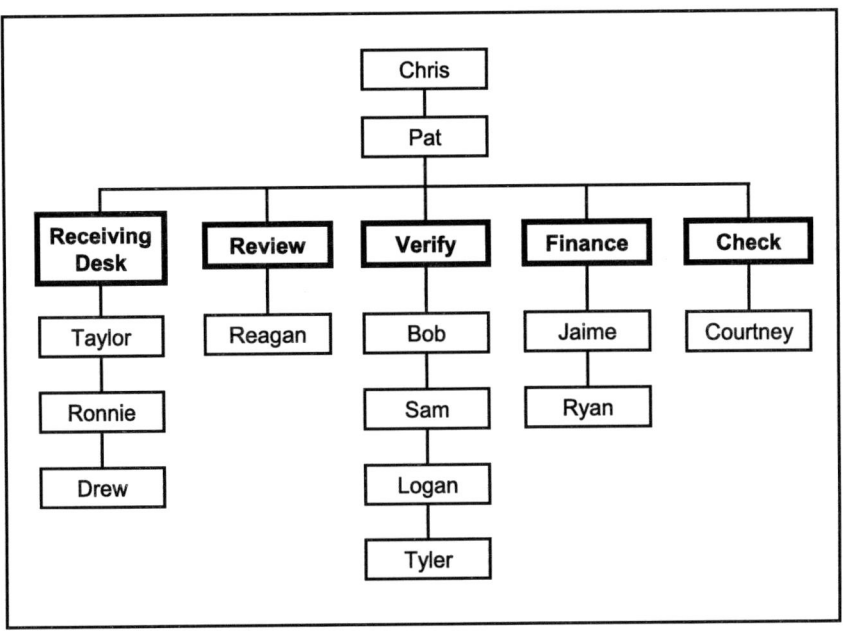

I assembled my materials in the conference room and waited for people to arrive. "Good morning," I said, as everyone made their way into the room and situated themselves. "I'm sure you all know we had a problem with the Mercy Hospital claim last week. And I heard from Chris that our track record for timeliness is trending downward. We're on the bubble now, at risk of losing customers, and we need to examine our procedures to improve our delivery reliability." Objective stated, now nail the scope.

"And, as if that wasn't enough, Chris has tasked us with improving claims processing for *all* our customers. Whatever changes we make must be global so they impact everyone, not just Mercy Hospital and our other major accounts. I'm not sure we can do all of that, so we're going to focus first on fixing our big customers. I'm hoping that'll satisfy Chris." I almost couldn't believe I said that last part out loud. "Once we square them away, we'll investigate what it'll take to incorporate all our other clients, too. Any questions?"

I intended to pause for an appropriate amount of time and then continue, but Taylor spoke up. "I'm not sure what more we can do for even a *few* of our customers, let alone the major ones, or all of them. We already made improvements to the system months ago. What more does Chris want?"

"I don't know yet," I admitted. "But I know we have to find a way. We can't afford to start losing clients. We've made some good improvements recently, but we need to see what else we can do." Scope done, now on to strategy.

"Here's what I want to do," I said, addressing the entire group. "I want to review the steps a claim goes through in our entire department and what happens along the way. If we're going to fix anything, then each person needs to know how they fit into the bigger picture. So, I want you all to briefly explain the activities involved at your step. Nothing too detailed, just a quick overview. Once that's done, I want you to talk to me about the problems you're having, then I'll develop a plan to present to Chris tomorrow."

I distributed the copies of the departmental organizational chart I had brought with me and gave everyone time to look at it. "Alright, are there any questions?" I asked. "None? Okay, then what's the first step in processing a claim?" I added that it might be the receiving desk and drew an oval on a flip chart titled "Receiving Desk."

Taylor spoke up. "Yes, we get it first. Me, Ronnie, or Drew, that is. A claim starts here when we receive it from the customer. That could be from a hospital, like Mercy, or from clinics, pharmacies, private practices, nursing homes, or even individual patients. As we all know, the information is usually incomplete, so we often have to contact the customer.

"Typically, customers are hard to reach, and they generally don't understand what information we need or are reluctant to talk to us. Sometimes our terms are too technical or they're worried they might be getting scammed. It can take a while to get everything we need but once we have it, we put our packet together for Reagan at Review."

"Thanks, Taylor," I said as I jotted down some notes. "Ronnie, Drew, anything to add?"

They both shook their heads, so I went on. "Okay, where do claims go once they're released from Receiving?"

"They go to me," said Reagan, "over at Review."

I drew a second oval, lower and to the right, and wrote "Review" in it.

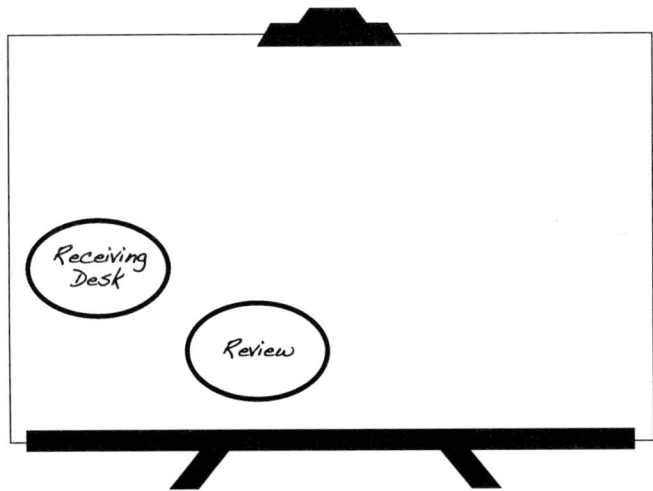

Reagan continued. "I get the packet from the folks at the Receiving Desk and then make sure the policy is valid by plugging the information into the system. I confirm it's still enforced, active, and up-to-date. If information is missing or incomplete, I have to give the packet back to

Receiving so they can take care of it. But, if the packet has already gone back and forth between us a few times, I might just send it on its way."

"Okay," I said, making some mental notes. "And where do they go after that?"

"They go to Verify," said Bob, "where either me, Sam, Logan, or Tyler handle them."

I drew another oval to the right of Review and labeled it "Verify."

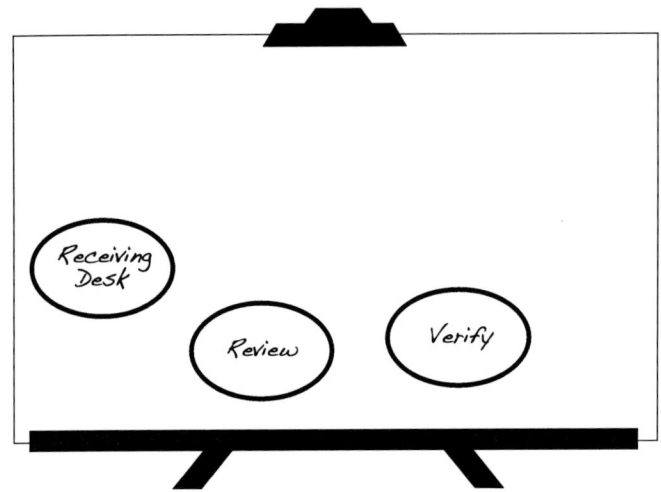

Bob continued. "Essentially, we have to make sure a claim falls within the scope of the policy, so we compare the two. Then, we interpret the claim – who was involved, what was done, when, where, by whom, etc. – to see what's covered. There's a lot of ambiguity in what we see, and sometimes we have to acquire more information or double-check what's there, which only further delays things. And, of course, we have to document everything we do in case a claim is challenged after we're done with it."

"Thanks, Bob," I said. "What's next?"

"Ryan and I pick it up from there in Finance," said Jaime.

I drew an oval above and to the right of Verify and wrote "Finance" in it.

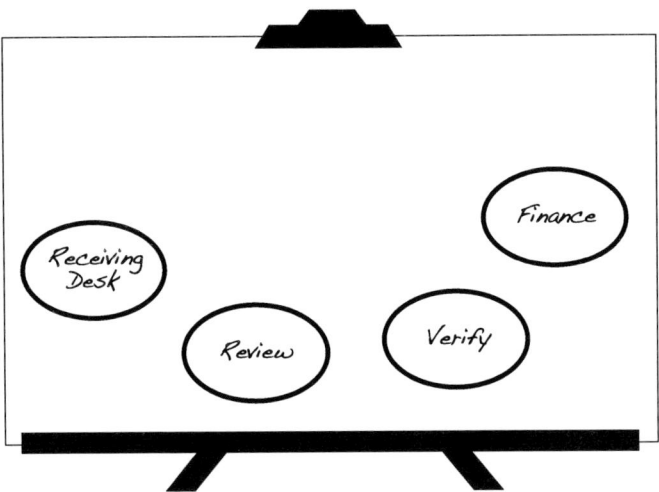

Jaime went on. "Once we get everything from Verify, we have to enter some numbers manually into the system, which then calculates the payment. And, anything that's considered a large payment is manually double-checked before the payment is made."

"Thanks, Jaime," I said. "And last but not least, we have Check." I drew the final oval above and to the left of Finance, and then an arrow to indicate the direction in which claims travel.

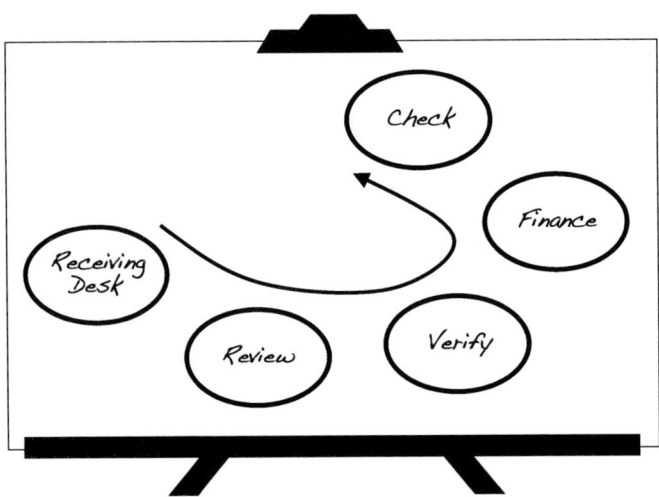

"Yup, that's me," said Courtney from the back of the room. "I enter the information into the system and then the checks get printed, stuffed, stamped, and mailed without me or anyone else ever touching them. That's the end of the process. The claim is complete at this point."

"Okay, thanks Courtney," I said. "Now that everyone knows what everyone else does, I want you all to talk to me about any problems you've been having. Don't hold back. Tell me anything that causes you pain during the course of a normal day, including why you think Mercy Hospital got delayed and why you think our trend in timeliness is heading south. I'm going to write your thoughts on the whiteboard and then use them to create a plan to fix all this. Any questions?"

Everyone looked at one another, but no one offered anything, so I jumped in. "Then let's start with Taylor, Ronnie, and Drew at Receiving. Talk to me about your problems, what happened with Mercy Hospital, and, more generally, why you think we might be trending late."

I went around the room to each department and wrote down their thoughts on the flip chart. It took most of the morning and early afternoon, but once everyone had said their piece, I thanked them, adjourned the meeting, then contemplated the list we created. Based on my knowledge of each department and the additional information they had given me, I added each department's current practice. (See chart at right.)

I sat at the conference table and stared at the flip chart. Where do I start? I need to come up with a plan I can present to Chris, one that will be satisfying, convincing, and deal with our major customers. Even though Chris wants to involve all our customers, I want to make progress on this, and I think including every customer will be like trying to boil the ocean. So, I'm going to focus on our major customers, including Mercy Hospital, and hope that's enough for now.

It was getting late. I grabbed some leftovers from the cafeteria downstairs and brought them back to the conference room so I could continue working. While I ate, I reviewed the department issues from the meeting. There were a lot of them, and any number might be causing us to miss our promise dates. There also seemed to be lots of commonality and overlap between some of the departments. I finished my food and decided

The Office That Grows Your Business

Receiving Desk Issues
- Incomplete information
- Illegible information
- Too much information, which requires additional sorting and filtering to get at the actual information that's needed
- Communication issues – language barriers due to technical terminology specific to our claims processing procedures
- Unpredictable changes in priorities
- No assigned maintenance of community equipment – fax paper, printer cartridges, toner, and speed dial numbers are not regularly maintained by anyone
- **Current Receiving Desk Department Practice** – Selective claim processing. Doing the easy ones first, or the ones with the most complete information, and saving the harder ones for later.

Review Issues
- Subjective approvals, decisions, and interpretations of claims
- Incomplete information, which causes returns to the Receiving department
- Delays of one day up to one week because of incomplete information
- Daily changes in what to work on next
- **Current Review Department Practice** – Send ambiguous or incomplete claims back to Receiving, or sometimes send them to Verify if they've already bounced back and forth a lot.

Verify Issues
- Incomplete information
- Delays of one day up to one week waiting for information or clarification from the claim submitter, which could be a doctor, patient, hospital, etc.
- Subjective approvals, decisions, and interpretations of claims
- Changes in priorities
- Communication issues – customers lack trust because they are suspicious of scams. They require us to validate our identity.
- Communication issues – language barriers due to technical terminology specific to our claims processing procedures
- **Current Verify Department Practice** – Double check information before starting to process a claim, and obtain missing information as needed from the claim submitter.

Finance Issues
- No existing standard for system maintenance
- Frequent priority changes
- **Current Finance Department Practice** – Manually validate and double check large payments.

Check Issues
- Unscheduled maintenance of equipment and supplies
- **Current Check Department Practice** – Follow security procedures for paper products and scrapped or voided checks.

to try to group the issues by their similarities, figuring this might help shorten the list into something more manageable.

> **Possible Reasons Why We Are Trending Late**
> *(condensed from morning meeting)*
>
> 1. Frequent reprioritization.
> 2. Claims forwarded to the next operation with incomplete, erroneous, or illegible information.
> 3. Too much information, which requires additional levels of filtering to get to the information that's actually needed.
> 4. Lack of communication with customers due to their lack of understanding of technical terminology and/or suspicions of our motivations because of scams.
> 5. Delays in common area equipment servicing.

This looks good, I thought to myself. It hits the highlights and gets to the heart of the matter, and concisely identifies what's causing us pain. It certainly seems like these are the main culprits for our downward trend in timeliness. I felt a degree of control return to my efforts, and I smiled for the first time today. I finally felt like I was getting somewhere.

It was near quitting time, but before I left, I wanted to update Chris on my investigation. Even though I didn't have too much to report at this point, I felt my narrowed list of possible reasons would demonstrate that I had made some headway and was zeroing in on a solution, which I intended to find tomorrow.

I gathered my things, tore the page off of the flip chart, and headed to Chris's office. I knocked on the door, stood in the threshold, and said, "Hey, Chris. I'd like to update you on what's been going on since we met this morning. Got a minute?"

"Sure, Pat," came the response. "Come on in. I'll feel better knowing what's happened today."

"Okay, here's a list of my findings," I said, handing over the page from the flip chart.

Chris reviewed it for about thirty seconds before saying, "So, it all boils down to this? These are the reasons you came up with for the downward trend in timeliness?"

"Yes, I believe so," I said. "I plan to think about it a bit more this evening, but what you have in your hand is a summary of the problems the associates are experiencing. I'm sure if we get rid of most of them, productivity will increase and the downward trend in timeliness will be reversed. It'll be tough, and we may have to phase-in the changes over time, but that's what I'm going to figure out tomorrow. Then, I'll develop an implementation plan and present it to you at about one o'clock tomorrow afternoon, if that's acceptable."

Chris pondered what I'd said, started to speak, stopped, gazed at my list of reasons again, and then replied, "I'll be interested to see that implementation plan, Pat. I don't see a lot of difference between your list here and what I experienced years ago. Some of these issues will be difficult to correct because they involve outside sources: customers, patients, doctors, etc. However, I agree that if each department eliminates their problems, you might see an upward trend."

Nothing new here? Is that what I just heard? These problems haven't changed over the years? Then what was done to reverse a downward trend in years past? These questions gnawed at me. I finally just said, "Thanks for the encouragement, I think," and faked a smile as I made for the door.

"Oh, and one o'clock tomorrow's a problem," said Chris. "I have a meeting that will last until one thirty, so let's start then."

"That's fine," I replied, grateful for the extra thirty minutes to prepare. "See you tomorrow." I made my way out of Chris' office and left for the day.

When I got home, I set my alarm for earlier than normal and fell into bed. I wanted to get an early start tomorrow so I could make as much headway as possible before meeting with Chris. I don't recall falling asleep, but the next morning, I don't recall feeling refreshed either.

Chapter 3

The Game Plan

I arrived at the office early Tuesday morning, got situated, and pondered the list we created yesterday. I need to come up with solutions to all five problems on this list, and it isn't going to be easy, I thought. I started making notes for counteractions and corrections for each reason. After spending most of the morning sifting through everything, I had developed a plan I felt comfortable presenting to Chris later in the day.

The Plan

1. Problem: Frequent reprioritization.

   Solution: We're going to continue with the current expedite policy, but we'll ensure that our major customers are routinely given a higher priority than everyone else by using a color-coded system. Each file folder will be noted with a color based on an established hierarchy. The top five major customers will have a unique color. Another color will be reserved for expedited claims, and all remaining customers will share a common color. This system can be implemented immediately and on a running basis. Within two weeks, all work in process should have a color associated with it and be prioritized accordingly.

2. Problem: Claims forwarded to the next operation with incomplete, erroneous, or illegible information.

Solution: Starting immediately, we will begin to chart the number of send-backs with each associate's name. We will establish a policy that prevents a claim folder from advancing to the next department unless all the information is completed correctly and legibly. We will need to do extensive training to make sure all personnel, in all departments, can accomplish this and catch mistakes and omissions. The timeframe for this is about six weeks.

3. Problem: Too much information, which requires additional levels of filtering to get to the information that's actually needed.

   Solution: With today's technology, we believe we can scan every document into an optical character reader, then have the computer look for the information that's needed, rather than have an associate read through the entire document. We'll need to review the options for a fast and accurate scanner, debug the system, and then make sure it's able to find the specific words we need it to, so it's a four-month project.

4. Problem: Lack of communication with customers due to their lack of understanding of technical terminology and/or suspicions of our motivations because of scams.

   Solution: We will come up with a scripted introduction that will put the customer at ease and assure them we are not trying to deny any claim. We expect to have a psychologist edit the script to make sure we are instilling confidence. Then, we will use a translator to convert our insurance-speak into requests an average person can understand. To do this, we will need to create the translator vocabulary. It will take about a month to research what is currently understood by the public, what colloquial terms apply, and then get the dictionary built. Then, it will take nine months to get it into our software. In the meantime, with some training, the associates can act as translators.

5. **Problem: Delays in common area equipment servicing.**

Solution: We will need some training here, too. I expect we can get the OEM to do some, and perhaps even recommend a system to ensure we always have the supplies we need to keep working. We can't be the only company that has this problem, so we might as well talk to the experts and see if they've dealt with similar situations elsewhere.

SUMMARY: Although some of these measures will require extensive training, monitoring, creation of information, and dependence on outside help, and many are long term, they should all ultimately simplify things. Until each measure is in place, we will depend on the colored priority system outlined in this list to ensure the satisfaction and retention of our major customers. This measure is the fastest and easiest to implement.

Okay, I thought, I'm ready for the meeting. I stood up and stretched, walked to the washroom to freshen up, and then headed to Chris's office. I gently tapped on the door and nudged it open.

"Hi, Chris. Are you available to review the corrective action plan?" I asked.

"Sure, Pat," came the reply. "Tell me how we're going to turn things around and support all of our customers. I could sure use some good news after the meeting I was just in." Chris selected a pen and a pad of paper and prepared to listen.

"Yesterday," I said, "I gathered everyone in the conference room and had them tell me the issues that were causing problems. This morning, I sat down and came up with solutions to them all. Here it is." And with that, I handed over my plan to Chris.

Chris took a look at it, dwelled on the first item for a while, and then said:

1. **"Inconsistent assignment and execution of priorities.** So, you're telling me that we're going to continue using the current priority

policy, but now with a color-coded scheme that will identify important customers and give them special treatment. And you can get this implemented within two weeks. Right?"

I was about to respond, but didn't get the chance. "Pat, there's no way this strategy will support all of our customers," said Chris. "It will obviously ignore some of our smaller customers, and in a very non-strategic way. Some of them are growing, and they have the potential to become our most profitable clients only a year or two down the road. You and your department don't have visibility into that. This policy could potentially make our service to these clients *worse*. This won't do. Let's move on to reason two."

I stood motionless. Already, this was not going well. My first item got shot down, and that was the key to everything.

Chris read aloud.

2. **"Claims forwarded to the next operation with incomplete, erroneous, or illegible information.** This is telling me your people won't advance a claim that has incomplete information, and you're going to track and chart who causes the most send-backs. You'll need to train people so they can recognize when information is missing or incomplete.

"I'm sorry, Pat, but this won't work either. If we measure how many claims get sent back by each individual, the associates will start selectively working on the easier ones and avoiding the harder ones. This measure will likely contribute to a *longer* overall processing time, not a shorter one. Next!"

This meeting is going faster than expected, I thought. Chris read the next point.

3. **"Too much information, which requires additional levels of filtering to get to the information that's actually needed.** You'll have all the incoming information scanned and let a computer determine what's important for processing a claim. Do you realize what that sounds like?"

Um, apparently not, I thought to myself. Chris went on. "If a claim has too much information on it, then I don't see how scanning it into a computer will help. Automated word search tools work for HR to eliminate resumes, but that's not our intention here. I don't think we'll save any time, and I think our service to our customers will actually decline and cause more problems...and we've already got plenty, Pat! Plus, what's the timeframe here? Will this really begin to resolve our problems in four months? What else do you have?

4. **"Lack of communication with customers due to their lack of understanding of technical terminology and/or suspicions of our motivations because of scams.** So, a scripted introduction will give us credibility and convince our customers we're on their side. And, we'll be able to get all the answers we need because we won't be using insurance-speak, so they'll have no trouble understanding our questions. That's what I'm getting from this plan, right? And we're going to add this vocabulary to the system software, too?"

The sarcasm was so thick I nearly suffocated on it. "Scripted introductions?" continued Chris. "I do like the idea of translating technical terms into street language, but I don't believe adding them to our software will solve our problems in a timely way. Besides, a nine-month timeframe is way too long. We need this done yesterday. Next.

5. **"Delays in common area equipment servicing.** The plan here is to have the local distributor manage the supplies, and teach us the simple stuff we need to know to keep our equipment functioning."

Chris put down the plan, looked up at me, and said, "I like the idea of having our local distributor and the OEM do some training and advise us on what other companies do to resolve the problems we're having. I believe that's called benchmarking. Maybe we could benchmark the equipment."

Without hesitating, Chris read through the summary and said, "Let's talk about extensive training. Who pays for it, and who minds the store while we train? We need to do it, I know, but it has to be done per some intended, controlled, and sequential impact plan. And, more importantly, this plan doesn't address how we're going to take care of *all* of our customers."

I might as well not have even attended this meeting, I thought. I didn't have a chance to reply to any of Chris's statements. It would've been nice to have been heard.

"Pat, I believe you lost sight of things when you decided to come up with solutions to the issues you and your team found," said Chris. "You came up with good answers to these isolated situations, but they make little impact on the overall problem. To me, the ideas in this plan read like random acts of goodness. Individually, each one has merit, but together, they don't make for an overall solution."

I nodded in agreement to show my understanding. Chris acknowledged the gesture and continued, "I can't accept this plan of action because it won't accomplish what we need. You're going to have to make some adjustments to address the needs of all of our customers.

"You need to look at the big picture, Pat. I think you've got a good grasp of the problem, so what should you do to get back on track? That's rhetorical right now. I suggest you spend the rest of the day and this evening thinking about it, and then we'll talk again tomorrow. Try to look at things from a higher level the next time around. See if that helps."

"Thanks, Chris," I said. "And…uh…thanks for the second chance. During your review of the plan, I wanted to disappear into thin air. But I was able to concentrate enough to recognize that what you were saying was, in fact, a fair assessment. Back to square one."

We acknowledged our mutual respect for each other, then I turned and left for my office. And for the first time ever, I was glad it wasn't the corner office. I'm not sure I could've performed an autopsy on someone's plan as precisely as Chris and still been responsible enough to administer fair criticism and not hold back on any of the deficient proposals.

I spent the rest of the day going over my plan again and attacking some of the backlog that had accumulated on my desk. After a few hours, I decided to leave. My mind seemed to be in a million different places.

As I packed my bag, I wasn't sure what I felt. Certainly, there was the disappointment of a rejected plan. I was also confused: how had I missed the target so badly? Chris had found little value in my plan and helped me understand it wouldn't fix anything. I was thankful to have been given a second chance to look at the big picture.

I headed out to my car, oblivious to the walk as I went over the last two days in my head, the information I had gathered, and how I might regroup. I couldn't tell you if I passed anyone in the lot, nor could I give you a single detail about the weather. I found my car, got behind the wheel, and buckled up. As I drove home, my mind was squarely focused on my own world of problems and what I might do to solve them.

Chapter 4

The Old Friend

It was still early Tuesday evening by the time I got home, but the week already felt like an eternity. I seldom had such stressful days – I wasn't accustomed to tackling a task where failure might be a realistic outcome – and I was drained of energy. I needed to clear my head so I could think outside the box tomorrow.

I was about to check the refrigerator for some leftovers when my cell phone rang. I didn't recognize the number displayed on the screen, which meant I probably didn't know the person on the other end. Should I answer it, or just let it go to voicemail? Ignore the phone and maybe they'll go away, I thought.

I looked over the contents of the fridge. Well, there's nothing too appealing, I thought, so I guess I'll go for takeout. My phone stopped ringing. At least something is working out as planned. Then, it rang again, and displayed the same number. Maybe it's important. I'd better get it. "Hello, this is Pat," I said.

"Hi Pat, this is Peyton," came the voice on the other end. "I wasn't sure I had the right number since I didn't get an answer on the first try. Are you in the middle of something, or do you have a minute to talk?"

"Oh, hi Peyton. It's you. I didn't recognize the number," I said. "What's up?"

"Well, I hate to interrupt your evening, but I have a career decision to make and I'd appreciate your advice. I was wondering if we could meet for coffee tomorrow morning before work. I remember you told me about your favorite spot on your way to work, and it isn't far from my commute.

Can we meet at seven? My treat."

That's all I need with everything that's going on, I thought. Something else to drain my brainpower. But I wonder what this is all about. "If you're buying, I'll be there," I replied, attempting to sound cheerful. "I'm actually just figuring out dinner for tonight so I can't chat now, but I'll see you tomorrow."

"Thanks, Pat. See you soon. Bye."

"Goodbye," I said as I hit the off button. I wonder what Peyton means by career decision. Maybe my recruiter has been active again.

I ran out and grabbed a pizza – veggie, for health's sake – and couldn't shake the feeling from the day as I crawled into bed, exhausted. As I drifted to sleep, my mind kept jumping to different events from the past two days. I wondered what Peyton would add to the mix tomorrow.

As Wednesday morning arrived and the sun cracked through a thick layer of clouds, I walked toward the coffee shop door, entered, and looked around for a remote place where Peyton and I could sit. I always liked to arrive first in any networking meeting so I could pick a seat with a good vantage point. As I checked for open tables, I noticed Peyton was already there.

"Hey, Peyton, you're early. And I see you already have your coffee. I'll get mine and be right back," I said.

"Hi, Pat. Good morning. Glad you could work this in. By the way, your coffee is already paid for, including Hazel's tip," replied Peyton, with a satisfied look.

I approached the counter, unsure of what to expect. The line was short, and when it was my turn, Hazel smiled and said, "The usual? Grande latte, two shots of espresso?" She continued doing the things baristas do to make the morning beverage. "Here you go, and it's complements of your friend. Enjoy."

"Okay, Peyton, I'm impressed. What did you have to do to arrange that?" I asked as I returned to the table.

"Well, it wasn't too hard to imagine you might be recognized here, so when I bought my coffee, I asked, 'Do you know what Pat always orders?' And they did, so I paid them handsomely to take care of you when you arrived," said Peyton.

"Clever," I said, as I sat and scanned the room for anyone I might know who could be a possible interruption. "So, what's the news? I've been wondering ever since you called."

"Well, I shared my career goals with you last week at the conference," said Peyton. "My plan was to become a technical expert on government tax law. Yesterday, my boss called me in and offered me a supervisory position in the Medicare/Medicaid group, which was my targeted objective. I guess my strategy didn't play out as I had planned, but I now have a shot at supervising the group that, I think, I want.

"I also recalled that you had the advantage of observing several management styles before you became a supervisor, and I haven't had that opportunity. I just want to know what you would recommend to help me succeed in this new position," said Peyton, with excitement and a hint of reservation. "I need to climb a steep learning curve to be able to supervise people the way I want. Are there any good seminars or books you can recommend? I've heard that peer groups can help, too. Are you familiar with any? What do you think about a career coach?"

I felt honored that Peyton was asking me for advice, but after yesterday, I was much less confident that I had anything worth sharing. "Well, first off, congratulations on being offered the supervisor's role," I said. "Are you going to accept it? I think you should go for it, but is there any downside?"

Peyton replied, "Yes, I'm going to take it. There's not really any downside, but I am a bit concerned because the performance bar has been set pretty high due to one of our company's other departments. They've been making improvements there over the past few months. I don't know much, but the bulletin board updates in the break room say they've really cut their lead time and improved their ability to meet their promise dates. You know, all that good stuff.

"I don't know if I'll be ready to do that in my group right off the bat, but I know my boss is watching those changes very closely and with a great deal of interest. Our marketing group indicates there's going to be a big increase in our Medicare/Medicaid market segment, which is why management agreed to add a supervisor. So, I'll be accepting a double challenge: learning to be a supervisor while trying to make a breakthrough in the way we perform. My boss has promised to support me, so I'm encouraged about that, at least."

I sat silently and pondered what Peyton said. A department cutting the time it takes to process claims *and* improving its ability to hit promise dates? What a coincidence! I wonder how they're doing this.

When I realized Peyton was waiting for a response, I said, "I recommend you take the position with enthusiasm, and mention to your boss you'd like to get some mentoring and training in management skills. Your company should offer that support for any internal change in position where different skills are expected. But, most of all, keep your head up and your eyes open to see the big picture at all times." Do as I say, not as I do, I thought.

After another pause and some more contemplation, I decided to confess. "I have to be honest. I don't really feel too qualified to give advice this week. I'm in the middle of a department trend that's headed south. I can tell you all about assuming a different position, adapting to a new role with associates that used to be peers, and administering management policy. Been there, done that. But, when performance trends need fixing, apparently, I'm still a novice.

"Things aren't going well at my office. We had a big problem last week while you and I were at that conference. My boss had to get involved and expedite a claim, and it was *still* late. The incident triggered a request for a report from IT, which revealed that our trend in timeliness is bad and getting worse. I got called on the carpet to provide a corrective action plan, which got shot down yesterday. So, I'm back to square one. Like you, I'm determined to find a way forward, but I don't have a clue where to start – at least not yet. That's my challenge for today."

"Wow, now I *am* concerned about taking this position. What if I find myself in your shoes? Then what? You'd better figure it out quickly so I can just copy you," replied Peyton, with some levity.

"Well, it sounds like your boss has been watching the improvements in that other department, probably knows the details of their progress, and will provide you some assistance in your own efforts. I'm sure you'll be fine," I reassured Peyton. "Perhaps I'll get *my* answer from what *you* implement, so *you'd* better learn fast!"

"I wish I could help you," said Peyton.

"Hey, this is your treat, and your meeting. We should spend the limited time we have discussing your opportunities," I said. "Then, I have to get back to reality."

Peyton sat quietly for a few moments and then said, "I have an idea. Let me ask my boss about the things they did in that other department, and I can let you know how they changed their trend. It's the least I can do."

"I appreciate the help. Thanks, Peyton. And thanks for the coffee," I said, feeling optimistic. "If others are making improvement, it's possible at my company, too. Speaking of changes, congratulations again on your new position. It seems like it's what you want to do so it sounds like the right move. It's going to take a lot of effort, but you appear willing to make it work and learn as you go. And you have a savvy boss who'll support you with what you need."

We simultaneously stood, moved toward the exit, and separated, each to our own vehicle. While still within hearing range, Peyton reiterated, "I'll talk to my boss and call you later today."

"Thanks," I said. "That'd be great. Whatever you can share is appreciated."

Peyton disappeared from sight as I carefully placed the remaining coffee in my cup holder, got into my car, and headed to work. Soon enough, I found myself in the parking lot, sandwiched between the usual meld of clustered cars. I gathered my things and made my way into my building.

I was excited about what Peyton told me and was looking forward to what I might find out later in the day. However, I didn't know how much I could count on that for today's meeting with Chris. What if Peyton can't convey the plan that department used? It can't be simple, and maybe it's even proprietary. It would be really frustrating to know a solution exists, but I can't have access to it.

I rode the elevator to my floor, stepped off, and decided to check in with Chris before beginning the day. "Morning, Chris," I stated as I got to the door. "I'll check back with you mid-morning if that's okay. I have some reviewing to do before we meet again to discuss how to improve the timeliness for all of our customers. Does that work for you?"

"Can we make it later in the morning, maybe even after lunch?" replied Chris. "My boss has asked me for a quarterly report this morning, and I'm not sure how long it's going to take to put together, especially since it's not the end of the quarter. I need to project the last month, which sounds a lot like guessing to me."

"No problem, I'll be plenty busy on this project. Let me know when you're ready," I replied. I left and went to my office. I unpacked my bag, sat at my desk, took a deep breath, and decided to look at the big picture.

Where did I go wrong? Most importantly, I didn't have confidence that we could improve the entire customer base, so I narrowed the scope to our major customers. With all our customers now in mind, maybe I should look at my list of reasons again and reevaluate them. I'm not sure this will be any more strategic than what I did yesterday, but it's a starting place at least. And I'm not really sure what else to do at this point.

I spent some time poring over the list of reasons I had generated, but after an hour or so of thinking about it, I didn't feel like I was getting anywhere. I went down to the cafeteria to grab a snack, and when I got back to my office, the phone was ringing. The number on the screen was not familiar to me, and I debated whether I should answer. Curiosity prevailed, so I accepted the call.

"Hello, this is Pat," I said.

"Hey, Pat, this is Peyton. Do you have a few minutes to talk? I have something I think you'd like to hear."

I'm glad I answered my phone! "Sure. But first, did you accept the offer?" I asked.

"Yes, I did, but that's not why I'm calling. I spoke to my boss about the department that's making all the improvements. It's claims processing for our industrial market. Different than what you do, but similar enough, I suspect. They handle policies that include buildings, liability, fleet insurance – stuff like that.

"I asked if I could get some understanding of what they did to improve their performance so I could share it with you. And, get this: I was told that I had been invited – actually, *expected* – to become familiar with their efforts because they want me to duplicate the results in the Medicare/Medicaid group. How about that!"

"That's great," I replied, feeling a bit deflated. Waiting for Peyton's report wasn't going to help me in a timely fashion. "Did you find out what they do differently?"

"No, not yet. There's a good news, bad news element to this call," Peyton replied, now sounding less enthused. "First, the bad news. I tried to find out what changes they made so I could relay the information to you. My boss told me they were all common sense changes, but would take too long to explain. Instead, he arranged for me to spend some time in that department to see for myself what they do differently there, which will then be followed by training and some mentoring."

"Good for you," I said. "I guess I *will* have to learn everything from you but, unfortunately, not soon enough. I still don't have any insight on what to do here."

I was really disappointed. If a department could accomplish such a turnaround, then there had to be a strategy that worked – and it might be applicable to my situation. I desperately wanted to know what they did, and I thought Peyton would be able to tell me. Gathering my emotions, I continued. "So, you mentioned a good news element, too. Care to elaborate on that?"

"Oh, that's right," said Peyton. "I did, didn't I? What do you have planned for tomorrow? Can you break away from your work to accompany me on the orientation? The group feels very confident about their progress and is willing to act as a benchmark for other companies. I asked if you could join me and, since our companies don't compete in the same market, both my boss and the industrial market department manager agreed to have you come. They think it'll be good for the associates in the department to talk about the differences between how they do things now and how they used to do them. They feel they'll gain confidence in their progress and actually recognize how far they've come. Can you make it?"

"Wow! Give me a minute to understand this offer," I said. "You're telling me that tomorrow, I'm going to be allowed to enter your company and participate in a benchmarking tour, where I'll learn about the changes your industrial market department has made, bring that knowledge and information back with me, and then apply it? Is that what you're asking? What do I have to do to participate? Do you want my firstborn, or what? Yes, of course I want to go, but I'll have to clear it with my boss. When do you need to know?"

Peyton replied, "Actually, I anticipated that you would be coming, so I tentatively committed for you. You should come by at 8:00 a.m. tomorrow. I'll give you directions later. When you get here, go to the front lobby, sign-in, and someone will come out to meet you. The tour could take the whole day.

"We're counting on you asking a lot of questions. With you probing to understand how and why things have changed, the associates will have to explain it to you, and they'll better realize their own understanding. So we gain from this as well."

"Thanks," I said. "I'll let you know if there's some reason I won't be able to make it, but I can't imagine what could keep me away. If needed, should I call you at this number or your cell?"

"Call my cell," replied Peyton. "I carry that with me, and I don't expect to be spending much time at my desk in the next two weeks."

"Thanks, Peyton," I said. "I owe you one. I sure am glad we met up at that conference last week."

Wow, I was delighted! This could be the breakthrough I need to get things moving here. I *have* to do this tomorrow, no question. As I was musing over my newfound fortune, I suddenly realized that Chris needed to know about the plan and agree to it. I began to generate a document that would illustrate the importance of this opportunity. It took some time, but when I was done, I had something I was confident would do the trick.

It was near enough to when we were supposed to meet, so I printed my document and headed to Chris's office. I stopped in the doorway and waited to be noticed. After a moment, Chris looked up and said, "Hi, Pat. I was just thinking about you. How's it going? Have you made any breakthroughs?"

I blurted out, "My new plan is to copy another company's success."

Well, nothing like cutting to the chase.

Chris looked as surprised as I felt. "Let me try that again," I said.

I handed Chris the document, then realized I did the same thing yesterday before promptly losing control of the meeting. Determined to be a participant in this one, I said, "Let me take you through the list and offer my thoughts as we go."

Not waiting for approval, I began to read.

1. "The original plan didn't work, because:
   a. We lost sight of the big picture.
   b. We had the wrong scope and focused only on our major customers."

I stopped reading the list and added, "So, the scope was inappropriately limited because I wasn't confident we could accomplish what we need to. I've changed my thinking about that, and realize we're going to have to figure out how to handle all of our customers."

I allowed just enough time for Chris to read number two.

2. I reviewed my list of reasons, but I was unable to come up with any additional insights.

I continued, "Last week, I attended a conference and revived an old college acquaintance. Some would call that good luck, knowing what followed." Then, I read item three aloud.

3. "A networking contact of mine knows another company with similar processes to ours where they've made great progress in both the time it takes to process claims and their ability to hit their promise dates.
   a. We can determine how feasible it is for us to implement a similar process. Can it be done here?
   b. Tomorrow I will be allowed to benchmark that company's processes and gain exposure to what they do."

Chris reviewed the remaining points.

4. I have no other alternatives at this point. I am still stumped.
5. What are your suggestions?

I commented, "Note that item four strongly suggests number three. I'm now looking for your input."

Chris sat back with a smile, then said, "What do you want me to say at this point, Pat? I agree you have a great opportunity to benchmark another company. There's no crime in copying what works."

"So, I have your approval to go tomorrow?" I asked, a little surprised.

"Yes, most certainly," said Chris. "I hope you find something there you can bring back and apply. But, if you don't, we can discuss other options. Pat, I have confidence in you. That's why I hired you eight months ago, and that's why I'm keeping you on this project."

"Thanks, Chris," I said. "Anything else?"

"Nope," came the reply, "that'll do it. Let's meet on Friday to review what you find tomorrow."

"Sounds good," I said. "See you then."

Now *that* was a good meeting, I thought as I left the room. I was able to participate, and Chris was supportive. I guess I tend to be more convincing when my arguments have some substance to them. I'd better let Peyton know I'm confirmed for tomorrow.

I called Peyton's cell phone and got no answer, so I left a voice message stating I would be in the lobby by 8:00 o'clock on Thursday morning. Later that afternoon, Peyton called back to let me know the best route to the company considering the construction, traffic patterns, and road conditions. It was a nice touch, and it left me feeling upbeat at the end of the day. I packed up, grabbed my driving directions, and left the office, excited for the day ahead.

Chapter 5

The Fateful Day

The alarm-clock rang with its usual annoying interruption, but I was in a very light slumber and welcomed the command to get out of bed. I'd slept well, but in heavy anticipation of what was to come today. I had to admit, I was excited about what I might discover.

Methodically, I executed my morning routine and headed out the door. I really didn't know what to expect today, but if that department Peyton talked about truly improved its performance, then I should to be able to learn some of what they did and implement it back at my office.

These people process industrial claims, I thought. That can't be as difficult as medical claims. I'm sure we have more clients, more procedures, and – because we deal with individuals rather than businesses – more incorrect or missing information. But hopefully there will be enough similarities that I'll end up learning something of value.

I arrived at Peyton's company, parked in the visitor's space, locked my car, and found my way into the lobby. Nice place, I thought. I noticed the LED monitor on the wall scrolling information about the company, the weather, associate announcements, and then my name on the welcome screen. Impressive, especially since I'm not even a paying customer.

I approached the sign-in desk, where I was greeted in a friendly tone and asked if I was Pat Peterson. After confirming, I signed in and received a visitor's badge. The receptionist then placed a call and informed the person on the other end that their visitor had arrived.

Shortly after, a woman approached me with an extended hand. We shook and she introduced herself as Jennifer Carrson. She informed me she was the continuous improvement manager and would be escorting me to the conference room to meet up with Peyton, then the three of us would spend the day learning about the system they had implemented.

As we made our way down the hallway, Jennifer said they had chosen the industrial claims processing team to pilot their improvements. When I asked her why, she said, "Why don't we talk about that when we meet with Peyton?" I nodded and she continued. "Peyton told me you two reconnected at a conference last week and that you're experiencing some of the same problems we faced before we began to think differently about how we do things. Perhaps we can help."

I smiled for a second, and then reality kicked in and my expression changed. I explained, "Well, I hope so. But I came back to a bit of a mess when I got back from the conference."

Jennifer half smiled and said, "It always seems to happen that way, doesn't it? I used to never take more than a long weekend off for fear of what I would come back to. But things are a little smoother here so I was able to work in a trip to Florida for spring break with my family this year." Now she flashed a full smile.

"So why are things running smoother now?" I asked, waiting to hear the secret to their success.

"It's simple," came the quick reply. "We learned about true flow and figured out how to apply it to our business to create Operational Excellence. It requires a little different perspective on things. You'll find out about that along with Peyton this morning, then I have some people I want you to meet this afternoon – the ones who are actually doing the work. We'll discuss everything beforehand, but I think it's better if you also see the system for yourself and hear how it works from the people who operate it."

We left the lobby. As we walked, Jennifer pointed out directions to the conference area, as well as the locations of nearby break rooms, restrooms, and water fountains. Each of these areas was also clearly marked with international symbols. As we neared the conference room, I noticed the hallways were identified with team names and there were color-themed variations in certain clusters of cubicles. I didn't see any of the typical departmental names posted.

"Here we are," said Jennifer. "Good morning, Peyton. How are you today?"

"Hey, good morning, Jennifer. And to you too, Pat. Glad you could rearrange your schedule so quickly to be here. I know you'll have some good questions that I wouldn't even think of asking," said Peyton, with some nervous excitement.

"Good morning, Peyton. I have those questions right here, ready to start," I said, lifting my bag.

"We'll be starting in about five minutes. I have to retrieve some materials from the copy center. Make yourselves comfortable and feel free to review the agenda in front of you. There's some coffee, tea, and chilled water in the nearby break area, so help yourselves. And get ready to learn a new language," Jennifer said with a wry grin as she departed.

"A new language?" I said to Peyton as she left the room. "I was never good at foreign languages. I'm not even that good with English! I just need to know how to solve my problems. Am I on the wrong bus here?"

"Relax, Pat," said Peyton. "Last night, I was reading some material Jennifer gave me, and it implied that we're going to have to get familiar with a new way of thinking. I'm sure that's all she means."

As we were reviewing the agenda, Jennifer returned and seemed pleased.

"Great, I see you're already showing interest in what we'll be doing today!" she said. "Let's get started. The day's format will be structured, but informal, so ask questions whenever you find something confusing. We're going to build on each element we discuss, so it's important to grasp each step as we go through it.

"Pat, I understand you have department management experience and are currently trying to solve some problems, but with a different approach. I'm going to depend on you to point out the differences in our system, for the benefit of both you and Peyton. It's hard to appreciate some of the subtle contrasts without a reference point, so you can provide that baseline. Okay?"

"Sounds good," I said.

"Alright, let me give you some background on industrial claims processing," said Jennifer, and with that, she quickly summarized the background, problem, scope, and schedule of their project. It seemed their previous decline in performance was similar to what my department was currently experiencing. The management team had heard about Operational Excellence and decided to apply the principles in their worst performing area so their efforts would produce the greatest results for the overall business. The logic was that if they could achieve Operational Excellence there, it would be a model that could be used to teach the rest of the company.

Jennifer continued, "Peyton, you and Pat are probably going to hear some unfamiliar terms over the course of the day, but bear with me." She paused briefly, and then continued. "When this whole process started about four months ago, I didn't know much about continuous improvement or which companies were famous for being really good at it. I was something of a newbie. But I quickly got a solid education in the principles of Operational Excellence. Then it fell on me to educate the team that actually applied the methodology. After all was said and done, life got simpler and better for everyone, including the boss.

"Speaking of the boss, one of the first things we had to do was get our management group aligned, and that was no easy task. I found a great speaker on Operational Excellence who was appearing at a conference, so I convinced our CEO and other executives to attend the session. When they returned, they were so excited about what they heard they couldn't wait to get started.

"By this point, we all understood the end game of Operational Excellence, but we felt we needed some help getting started with the process. We found someone who was an expert in teaching Operational Excellence in the business process environment, and that office-specific knowledge enabled us to accelerate our success as opposed to performing random acts of goodness. That's where I got my education."

Random acts of goodness. That's not the first time I've heard that phrase.

"We might be on a journey," continued Jennifer, "but that *doesn't* mean we don't have a destination. Ours is Operational Excellence, and knowing where we were going enabled us to get there a lot faster. It was like we had a GPS device to always keep us on course. I believe we've accomplished more and come farther, faster in the past four months than many companies have in the past four *years*.

"What does that mean? Most companies see continuous improvement as using tools to get better every day, or they try to eliminate waste wherever they can find it." Jennifer went to the flip chart and drew a graph.

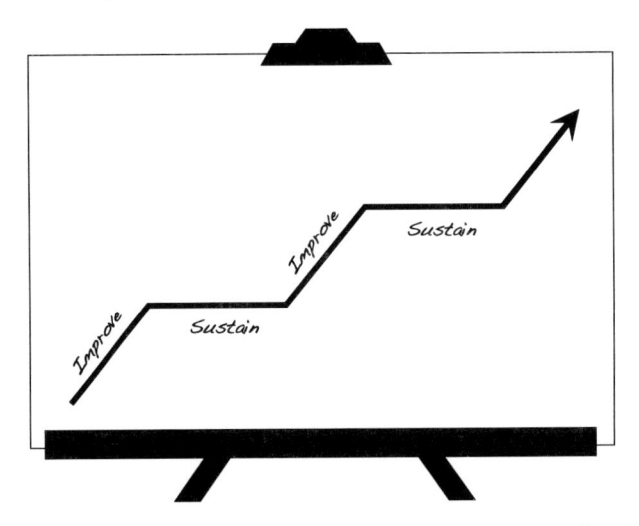

"Typically, we improve a little bit, then we sustain at that level. And we keep going like this. Don't get me wrong. It's all good, it just takes a long time." She drew another graph on the flip chart to illustrate her point.

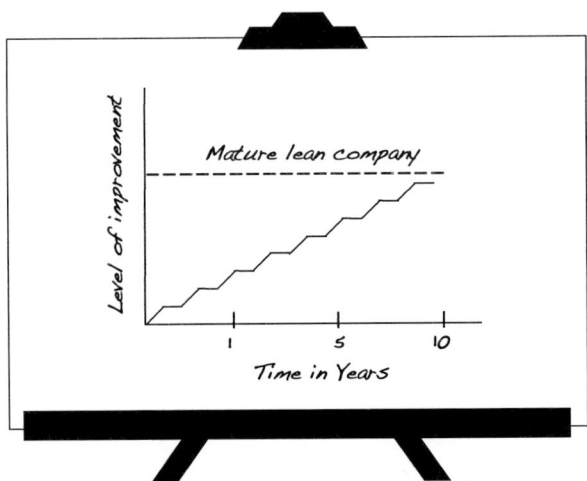

"But," continued Jennifer, "Operational Excellence raises the bar." Another graph came to life.

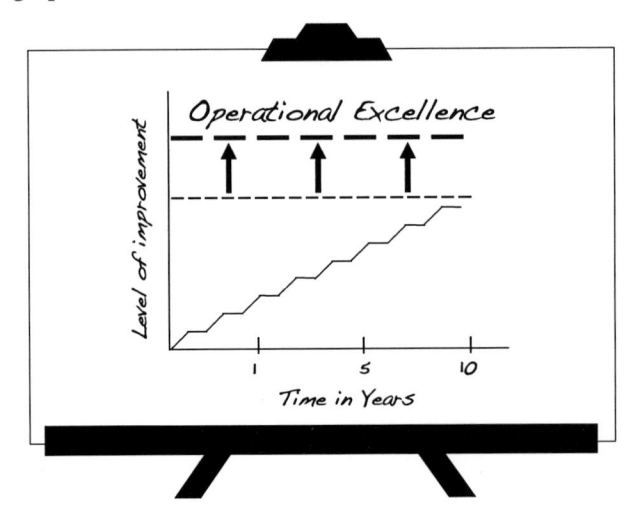

[Graph: Operational Excellence — Level of improvement vs. Time in Years (1, 5, 10), showing a staircase rising toward a raised dashed line with upward arrows]

"With Operational Excellence as our destination," said Jennifer, "we can do more, and do it faster, than even some of the best companies." She added a little more detail to the graph, and it became clear to me that we could go much farther, sooner by striving for Operational Excellence.

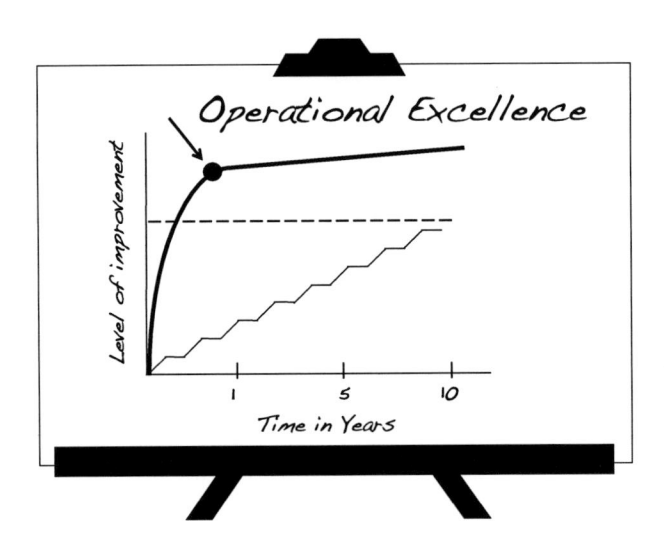

[Graph: Operational Excellence — Level of improvement vs. Time in Years (1, 5, 10), showing a steep curve rising quickly past the dashed line, compared to the slower staircase]

"Okay, hold on a second," said Peyton. "What exactly is Operational Excellence? You've mentioned it a few times now, and even said it's the destination of our journey. But how is Operational Excellence different from any other corporate catchphrase out there?"

"Yes, how do you define it?" I added. "We talk about Operational Excellence at my company. We even have a metrics board that measures safety, productivity, delivery, and customer satisfaction. It announces updates in our quality improvement programs, suggestions, rewards, recognitions, and numerous employment benefits for self-improvement."

Jennifer nodded and said, "I'll define Operational Excellence now since it's so critical to what we're going to be doing today. But the definition will probably have deeper meaning for you once you actually see Operational Excellence in action later, so you might want to write it down.

> **Operational Excellence** is when each and every employee can *see the flow of value* to the customer and *fix that flow before* it breaks down."sm

Jennifer used extra emphasis when she said "see the flow of value" and "fix that flow." She explained that the goal is to have value flow continuously to the customer, uninterrupted, and to have front-line employees be able to identify when the flow of value is starting to break down, step in, correct it, and get it back on track. I was a little confused at first, because I didn't know *what* we flow in the office, so I asked. Jennifer explained that we typically flow knowledge and information as opposed to something physical or tangible.

With that question out of the way, I thought about everything for a minute, and then it became clear. I could immediately see the power of Jennifer's definition of Operational Excellence. It was simple, easy to understand, powerful, practical, and applicable at all levels of an organization. These last two details were key. Since the definition wasn't just some lofty slogan, I could easily picture myself discussing Operational Excellence with front-line employees and upper management alike because it was something to which they could all relate.

"Alright," said Jennifer. "Now I want you both to imagine a world where you never have to worry about whether your jobs are on time, everyone is always working on the right thing, there are never any priority shifts, and your jobs always get out to your customers when they're supposed to. Oh, and by the way, all of your work flows through the office *without any management intervention whatsoever*. What would you say to that?"

Obviously, I was extremely skeptical of the scenario Jennifer described. It would be amazing if I could do any one of those things in my office, but to think of them all happening without management intervention – no way! I suddenly wondered if I was going to get anything useful out of today's session. Everything Jennifer just said sounded like pie-in-the-sky foolishness that couldn't be applied to the unique, complex situation I faced at my company.

"Well," I said, "I think I would say two things. One, everything you just described sounds amazing. And, two, it sounds like a total fantasy, especially the part about no management intervention."

"That's a natural reaction at this point, Pat, since we haven't covered much about Operational Excellence," replied Jennifer. "But I think it'll make more sense once I explain why it's possible for anyone to achieve Operational Excellence.

"Striving for and achieving Operational Excellence is not about having the right leader. It's about following the right process and using the right guidelines. We're not going to rely on personal opinions to get us there, or the decisions of managers. We're going to use a process, because a process can be taught to everyone, and good opinions cannot. That's why anyone can strive for Operational Excellence, in *any* environment, and make it happen.

"And, by using a process that we teach to everyone, we won't and don't need managers making decisions all the time. In fact, our managers won't have time, because with Operational Excellence, they'll be busy doing something else entirely. I'll talk more about that later but, for now, know that management has a very specific and important role to play when it comes to Operational Excellence, one that will benefit the entire business and keep them focused on what matters most."

I was now more intrigued. When Jennifer talked about striving for

Operational Excellence by following a process and not simply relying on effective or clever leaders, she got my attention. I've known too many people who worked at companies that were successful only because the leader carried a bigger hammer than everyone else. Then, when that person left, everything fell apart. But, if I could transform my office by teaching a process to everyone, I could create change that would last, no matter who left or joined the company.

"Okay," said Jennifer. "Today's all about getting an overview of Operational Excellence and what process you need to follow to achieve it in the office. I'm going to be brief, so keep in mind there's more to it than what I'm going to be able to get into today.

"To keep things relatively simple, we're going to take the definition of Operational Excellence and break it down into two parts. Remember, the full definition is 'When each and every employee can see the flow of value to the customer, and fix that flow before it breaks down.'

"Let's start with the first part of the definition about each and every employee seeing the flow of value to the customer. What do you think we should talk about first?"

"Well," I said, "it seems to me the first thing we need to discuss is value, what it is, and how we should define it. If part of Operational Excellence is flowing value to the customer, then we'd better know what we're talking about."

"Very good," said Jennifer, as she moved to the front of the room and stood by the easel. "So, what's value? What do you think?"

"Something worth paying for," Peyton answered. "If I'm a customer, then I'm willing to pay for goods and services that hold value for me."

"That's good, Peyton," responded Jennifer. "And actually really close. But we're after something a little more specific. When we talk about value in an office setting, we're referring to any business process *activity* the customer is willing to pay for[1]. Value was first coined in this way through its use in lean."

"How's that any different from what I said?" asked Peyton.

---

[1] Womack, James P. and Daniel T. Jones. Lean Thinking: Banish Waste and Create Wealth In Your Corporation. Simon & Schuster. New York, New York, 1996. Page 311.

"It all comes down to the word 'activity,'" said Jennifer. "The customer doesn't necessarily want to pay for anything and everything we do, only for the specific activities that generate a product or service for them. For example, the physical act of printing a check adds value, but meetings to talk about a customer's claims do not. Think of value as the actions, or verbs, in our business processes that the customer is willing to pay for. Anything that does not add value is waste. Bear in mind there are activities that do not add value, but that we have to do anyway due to technological limitations or legal mandates. Any questions on value?"

Neither Peyton nor I had any lingering uncertainties, so Jennifer went on. "Now that we know what we're talking about when we use the word value, we're going to go over a quick example that will illustrate the first part of our Operational Excellence definition and demonstrate how we're able to see the flow of value. Would you mind rearranging your seats for me?"

Jennifer had us sit side by side and then joined us at the conference table. Peyton was in the middle, I was on the right, and Jennifer was on the left. To Peyton's left and right, she put a large "X."

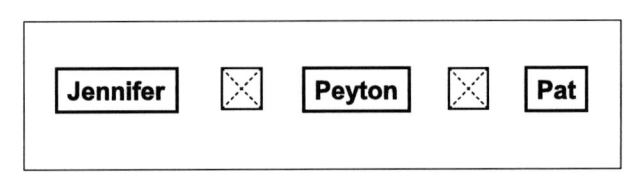

| Jennifer | ☒ | Peyton | ☒ | Pat |

"I have a number of documents that require your approval, which are these blank sheets here," said Jennifer. "Each of us will review a document to ensure the prior approval is legible, approve it by initialing it, and then place it on the 'X' to our right, where it will be picked up and processed by the next person. We can only place a job on the 'X' when the space opens up. So, if another job happens to be on the 'X' when you go to put yours there, you can't do it. It should only take about two seconds for each of us to sign our names. And Pat, when you're done signing yours, just pile up the sheets to your right. Any questions?"

Peyton and I understood what we'd heard, so we started the exercise. We worked silently for a short amount of time. By the time we finished, I had accumulated a fair number of documents to my right.

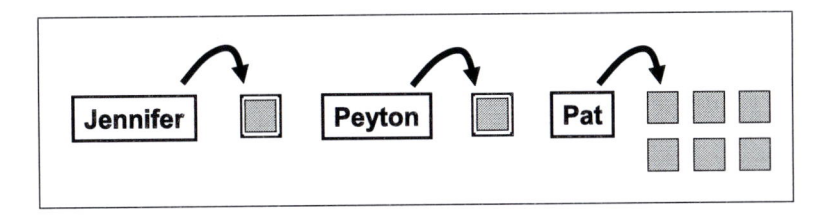

[Diagram: Jennifer → □ → Peyton → □ → Pat → □□□ / □□□]

"Alright, good job everyone," said Jennifer. "What we've just created is something called a continuous flow cell, or a one piece flow cell. In this type of setup, we operate in a make-one, move-one fashion. So, each person only works on one job at a time and, when they're done with it, they move it on to the next person.

"We're going to cover continuous flow in much more detail in just a bit but, for right now, I'm showing it to you for a slightly different purpose. Peyton, I need to ask you some questions about your role in the exercise we just did."

With that, Jennifer got up from her chair and proceeded to write five questions on the flip chart at the front of the room.

Five Questions for Business Process Flow

1. How do I know what to work on next?
2. Where do I get my work from?
3. How long should it take me to perform my work?
4. Where do I send my work once I'm finished with it?
5. When do I send my work once I'm finished with it?

"Peyton," continued Jennifer, pointing to the easel. "Can you answer all of these questions?"

After thinking about it for a few moments, Peyton responded. "Yes, I think so. Let me take them one at a time just to be sure. The first one's easy. I knew what to work on next based on whatever you handed me. For question two, I got my work from you. More specifically, I retrieved it from the 'X' on my left.

"For question three, you told us before the exercise started that it should only take about two seconds to complete a job, so that was clear. For question four, I sent my work to Pat. Specifically, I sent my work to the 'X' on my right, and Pat took it from there. And, for the last question, I knew to send my work when space cleared at the 'X' on my right."

"Very good!" said Jennifer. "See how easy that was? If we can correctly answer these five questions, then we have the basis for good flow. And, as long as one more condition is met, we're well on our way to achieving Operational Excellence: there can't be any managers, supervisors, schedules, or computer printouts telling each person what to do next."

That last statement caused Peyton and I to take notice, since it seemed unfathomable an office could ever work like that, but Jennifer continued. "Before you think I'm completely crazy, let me ask you this. How many managers, supervisors, or computer printouts did we need for our continuous flow cell to work?"

"None!" exclaimed Peyton, clearly delighted. The proverbial light bulb went on over my head, too.

"Exactly," said Jennifer. "Everything in the continuous flow cell happened without management intervention. None whatsoever. No one hovering over us, no reports telling us what to do next. And, since we don't need schedules, we don't have to spend time creating them. Imagine if your company could function as seamlessly as our continuous flow cell did." She paused to give us time to think about it.

I sat in my seat mulling over everything. With a clear example to reference, I now had a better understanding of what Jennifer meant earlier when she spoke of work flowing through the office without management intervention. But, something else was bothering me, so I spoke up. "I understand the exercise we just did, but I don't really see the point of it. It's way too simple. Nothing in the office, or at least my office, works like this. How is it supposed to help us?"

"You're absolutely right," said Jennifer, somewhat to my surprise. "The exercise *was* simple, but it was designed that way to illustrate a very specific point. First off, I'm sure you'd agree that Peyton answered all five questions satisfactorily, right?"

"Yes," I said, not really sure where Jennifer was going with this.

She continued, "And, I'm sure you'd also agree that the three of us operated successfully with absolutely no management intervention, right?"

"Yes," I said. "I'd agree with that, too."

"Good," she said. "Then you're one step closer to understanding what it is we're trying to achieve with Operational Excellence. This continuous flow cell worked because everyone in it was *connected* to one another. You, me, and Peyton were connected in *flow*, and we knew we had flow because we were able to answer those five questions. Additionally, we were able to function without management intervention of any kind. What we're going to do now is take the same concepts that made this whole thing work and expand them throughout the entire office."

"You mean we're going to seat everybody side-by-side?" I asked, incredulous.

Jennifer chuckled to herself before saying, "No, not quite. The goal will be for every employee in the office to be connected in flow, able to answer all five questions, and function without management intervention. But, since the office is much more complicated than the simple exercise we just did, the process we're going to use will be different and more involved. And that's exactly what we're going to get into next."

Chapter 6

The Education, Part I

Jennifer stood by the easel and said, "Like we talked about before, we're breaking down the definition of Operational Excellence into two parts. We've already talked a little bit about how to see the flow of value. But to do that, we need to have flow first, don't we?"

Peyton and I both nodded.

"Glad you agree," said Jennifer. "So, if you two were going to try to create flow in your offices, what would you do?"

I thought about it for a few moments before saying, "I'm not sure what you mean. It sounds like creating flow will make things better, so I think I'd just go about it in my normal way."

"And what way is that?" asked Jennifer.

"Well, I'd pull my team together in a room and do some brainstorming," I began. "After enough time and good ideas, we'd decide on the best ones and then make them happen."

"I thought you might respond with something like that," said Jennifer. "Most companies do just what you described, but that's *exactly* what we're *not* going to do. Brainstorming works great for some things, but not for creating flow and achieving Operational Excellence."

"You've got to be kidding," I replied in amazement. "We do a lot of brainstorming at my company. We want everyone's input and knowledge."

Jennifer didn't budge. "Yes," she said. "That's the common approach, and it's one of the major game-changers in Operational Excellence."

"Alright," I conceded. "If brainstorming is out, then what do we do?"

"I'm glad you asked," said Jennifer. "For the rest of the morning, I'm going to briefly describe the sequence of steps we applied to create flow in our office. Peyton, you'll get more in-depth training on this in the days to come, but for now, I just want both of you to be aware of the process we used.

"After we understand these steps, we'll go out into the office and observe them in action. I'll point out the areas that were transformed and give the associates a chance to explain how everything works and answer any questions you may have. The exercise will benefit everyone because when the associates explain what they do, they'll be reinforcing their understanding of Operational Excellence and building confidence in the new system. Let's get started."

With that, Jennifer went to the front of the room and stood by the easel. She picked up a marker and flipped to a new page. "We use eight guidelines to create flow in our business processes," said Jennifer. "I'll list them all, and so should you. I've found that writing things down helps people retain what they're learning."

She listed the eight guidelines on the page.

Business Process Guidelines for Flow

1. Takt Time (or Takt Capability)
2. Continuous Flow
3. FIFO
4. Workflow Cycles
5. Standard Work for Flow
6. Single Point Initialization
7. Visual Indicators
8. Changes In Customer Demand

"Like I said before," Jennifer added, "we're leaving out some steps that you must – I repeat – *must* go through if you're going to strive for Operational Excellence. But I won't go into them now because we don't have enough time. Plus, today we're just trying to get an understanding of the process and methodology involved.

"Okay, do you have the guidelines written down? These represent a disciplined, scientific, sequential approach to creating flow. We use the first five to design our flow, and we use the last three guidelines to determine how we're going to operate it.

"These guidelines are to be used in sequence, not as a menu. We can't just pick and choose which one to use, and we don't brainstorm. This will make more sense as I explain each guideline and show how they build on one another to create flow."

#1: Takt Time (or Takt Capability)

"Here's an analogy for guideline number one. Remember those old Viking movies, where two columns of husky men had oars and used them to power the boat? If you recall, they weren't at liberty to pull the oar whenever they pleased. They knew that the fastest way to move the boat in a straight line was if they all pulled together at the same time. To make this happen, their oar strokes were regulated by the beat of a drum. We're going to do something similar in our offices. Our first guideline is takt time, which is a word of German origin that means 'rhythm' or 'beat.' Let me explain the significance.

"Takt time is the rate of the customer demand and tells us the rate at which knowledge and information need to flow through our office. This concept may seem immaterial, overly simplistic, or not really applicable at this point, but it's the foundation of flow." Jennifer checked the expressions on our faces and determined that she could continue.

"Takt time is a reference number that we use to synchronize the pace of our office processes to the pace of customer requests. It's mathematically defined as the effective working time per period divided by the customer demand per period."

Jennifer went to the flip chart and wrote down the equation for takt.

$$Takt = \frac{\text{Effective working time per time period}}{\text{Customer requirement per time period}}$$

"By establishing this beat," she continued, "we can determine how frequently the customer is requesting work from us. When associates aren't able to sense this beat, which is typically the case, work moves sub-optimally through the office. Going back to the Viking analogy, if there's no beat, then everyone pulls their oars at different times, and the boat goes nowhere.

"For the moment, try to imagine what it would be like if each associate could finish his or her task at the same time, then pass it on to the next process at the same time, just like we saw a few moments ago in our exercise. The timing for all of this would be governed by a predictable and repeatable drumbeat, the speed of which would be how often a customer wants the service. Then, work would never have to wait between our processes. Now, I guarantee we *won't* be able to do this in the office because of the complexities we face there, but hopefully this example helps illustrate the purpose of takt.

"Here's how we compute our takt time," continued Jennifer, pointing back to the flip chart. "Peyton, how many effective working hours do we have in a day?"

"Theoretically, we're in the building nine hours per day, but many people are here for much longer," replied Peyton.

"Right, but how many of those scheduled hours do you actually spend working on specific jobs?" asked Jennifer.

"Well, we have an hour off for lunch," said Peyton, "and two ten-minute breaks during the day, which leaves seven hours and forty minutes for working. But we also stay late, work through lunch and breaks sometimes, and we're allowed to be absent for personal time. You did say *effective* working time, but I don't know if that means we should discount time for meetings, interruptions, priority changes, discussing current events at the coffee machine, or reading bulletin boards. What are you getting at?"

"Just that," said Jennifer. "In the office, there are plenty of things that pull us away from the work we're supposed to be doing. However, for the purpose of calculating takt time, we want to use the expected or scheduled time of seven hours and forty minutes. We don't factor in time lost due to meetings, fantasy football leagues, or anything else. We've got seven hours and forty minutes in a day, plain and simple."

"What's this for?" I interrupted. "I suppose we have the same amount of time available at my company, but my associates have other tasks to do each day besides processing claims. So, how do I determine the effective time for them? I mean, they might only work on claims for three or four hours a day."

"Good, I'm glad you brought that up," said Jennifer. "Let's go back to the mathematical definition of takt for some clarification. Takt is the effective working time per period divided by the customer demand per period. The associates here multitask as well, as they do in every office, but they're available for seven hours and forty minutes during the day. Perhaps we don't *use* all that time, or use it as well as we could or should, but that's the amount of time we have at our disposal and it's this amount of time on which the rate of customer demand is based."

Peyton and I looked at each other with a glance that confirmed we were only half convinced the previous discussion had been meaningful. Where's this going? I wondered.

"The other part of the takt time equation is the customer demand per period," continued Jennifer. "But that's a slippery number, and sometimes subjective. It may be relatively steady at your business, Pat, but here, it changes quite a bit. We can't just look at it for a day. We have to consider a longer period and then average it out.

"But there's another approach that's much more useful, and this is where capacity versus capability comes into play. Once we know the difference between the two, we can get down to how we practically apply the takt time concept in our office.

"Capacity is a measurement of how much volume we can produce over a given period of time. Typically, it's expressed as units/time. But, since capacity only speaks to volume, there's a limit to how useful it can be.

"A more complete and realistic approach is to describe our *capability*. This is a measurement of how much volume *and mix* we can produce over a given time period. The mix is the critical addition here, and it means the different types of jobs we might get from the customer. In this case, it's claims. We know that certain claims take longer than others. So, if the mix of claims changes, then it's going to affect how much work we can do in a day. Since capacity doesn't speak to mix, it ends up being a pretty meaningless measurement. But capability does speak to mix, and that's why we want to use it going forward."

"I still don't see how this really helps us," I said. "Even if we're able to determine our capability, we won't know exactly what our customers are going to request from us on any given day."

"That's an important point, Pat," said Jennifer. "Since, on any given day, we won't know exactly how many requests we're going to get from our customers, we want to establish not just one, but *multiple* capabilities, each of which accommodates a specific range of volume and mix we might get and has a unique drumbeat. This is something called *takt capability*. While we may not know the volume and mix we're going to get each day, we should be able to determine the volume and mix we're capable of *doing*. Because of the complexities we face in the office, we typically need to use takt capability instead of a straight takt time calculation.

"To do that, we need to look at our customer demand profile and then create different takt capabilities around it. However, we also need to look at the profile and see if there is significant variation or spikes in it."

Jennifer drew some quick sketches on the flip chart.

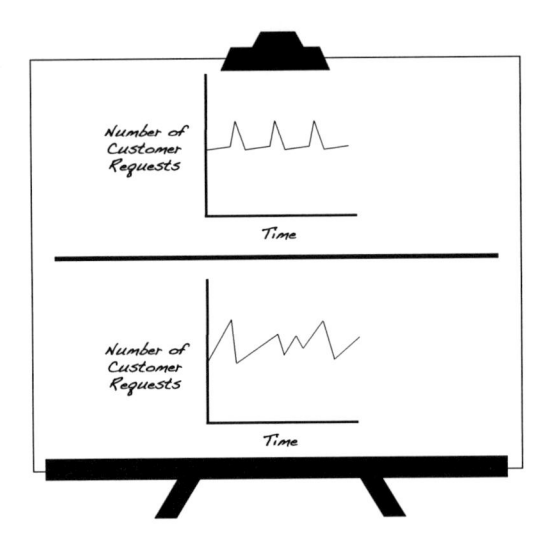

[Flip chart sketch: Upper graph labeled "Number of Customer Requests" vs "Time" showing spiky demand pattern. Lower graph labeled "Number of Customer Requests" vs "Time" showing more leveled but variable pattern.]

"For example, with industrial claims processing, we did some analysis and found that the greatest demand was always on Friday. Essentially, our demand profile looked like the one I drew in the upper portion of the flip chart. After some digging, we determined that this variation was self-induced. Some people were just waiting until the end of the week to flush their work to us. So, with a little education and communication, we were able to eliminate some of that variation. Now, we didn't remove *all* of it, since some was truly out of our control, and this is why we created a series of takt capabilities to respond to the different ranges of volume and mix we might get from our customers." Jennifer flipped to a new page and sketched a new drawing.

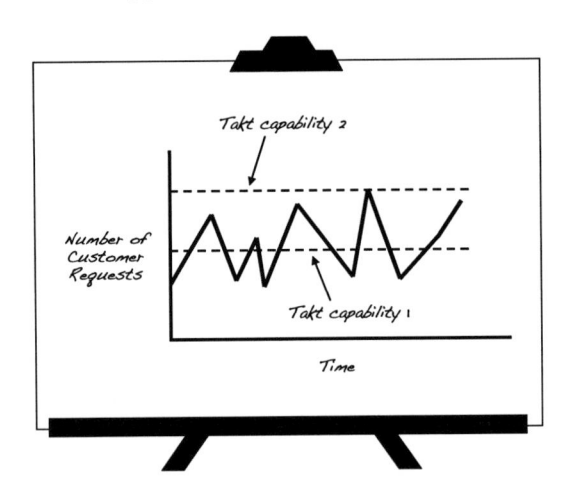

[Flip chart sketch: Graph of "Number of Customer Requests" vs "Time" with two dashed horizontal lines labeled "Takt capability 2" (upper) and "Takt capability 1" (lower), with a variable demand line crossing between them.]

Jennifer checked our body language and saw we were both still alert and following her. She continued, "Also, it's critical to note that we must review our takt capabilities periodically to determine if we need to recalculate them. If so, we might need to change the number of associates we employ or how much time they spend doing certain activities.

"This afternoon, on the tour, you'll see a system that shows our associates when their volume and mix of work has exceeded their takt capability, and you'll also see how they react and fix the flow before it breaks down – all *without* management intervention. That brings us back to Operational Excellence, but we'll save that for when we get to the second part of the definition.

"Now, let's do a little review, because takt time and takt capability are only the first of eight guidelines we have to cover. To begin, who wants to tell me about Operational Excellence?"

"Operational Excellence is where each and every employee can see the flow of value to the customer, and fix that flow before it breaks down," said Peyton.

"Good. So how does Operational Excellence relate to takt?" asked Jennifer.

I spoke up. "Takt defines the rate at which value needs to flow through the office to meet the expectations of the customer. It's a drumbeat that allows each associate to know when their task should be completed and moved to the next process. Without takt, each person ends up marching to the beat of a different drum depending on how he or she perceives the customer's needs and balances those with their own workload. It would be like an orchestra that let each instrument play at its own tempo. We wouldn't exactly end up with beautiful music."

"Good and comprehensive," said Jennifer. "Tell me about takt capability."

Peyton volunteered, "Takt capability describes how much volume and mix, not just volume, we can handle in a given time period. We use it because we typically don't know the number or types of claims we're going to get from the customer on any given day. We want to set up multiple takt capabilities so we can handle fluctuations in customer demand, and each one should have its own plan that describes how it operates."

"So, we use takt capabilities when we have variable demand or we don't know what our mix will be, right?" I asked.

"Yes," said Jennifer, "but there's also one more reason I haven't covered yet. Pat, remember when we were talking about calculating takt, and you mentioned that your associates may only work on claims for three or four hours a day? We have a term for these employees. We call them shared resources, because they share their time among many duties and responsibilities. In all the offices I've worked, every single associate was a shared resource. For this reason alone, we'll always end up using takt capability."

#2: Continuous Flow

Jennifer walked across the front of the room. She stopped and said, "Let's address the next guideline, which is continuous flow. We won't be able to cover all the details of this one today, but there are plenty of books out there that can help fill in the gaps for you.

"We saw continuous flow once before during our signature exercise when we demonstrated how to see the flow of value. Since most people in the office are shared resources and divide their time among many different duties and responsibilities, full-time continuous flow isn't really a viable option. But, we can have part-time continuous flow, where the associates involved all have the same amount of work to do, perform to a takt capability, and operate in make-one, move-one fashion.

"Let's think back to the exercise we did. What's it like in our offices now, when we don't have continuous flow?"

"Work piles up everywhere," I replied. "And not just at the end of the line like it did in the signature exercise. All those in-baskets on everyone's desks are filled to the brim with work that needs to get done."

"Good," replied Jennifer. "And what happens to the work while it sits in those in-baskets between everyone? Just to be clear, even though the in-baskets sit on people's desks, no one associate has ownership of the work in them. The work is in limbo. At that point, it doesn't belong to the person who put it there any more or less than it does to the person who will eventually take it. So, let me ask you this: what happens or can happen to work while it's sitting in someone's in-basket waiting to be processed?"

"Well, it can get sorted and shuffled," I offered. "And priorities might change. Sometimes, the work requires a more in-depth review because it's gone cold sitting for so long. Or, a customer's needs have changed, and we don't know it."

"All good responses, Pat, but I'll answer my own question to drive home the point," said Jennifer. "What can happen to work while it sits in an in-basket? Only two things: *anything and everything*. This uncontrolled flow is subject to everything you mentioned, and more. I think we'd all agree it does us no good for work to sit around waiting like this. Going forward, we're going to try to prevent this from happening, and continuous flow is how we're going to do it."

"I agree," I said. "But how are we supposed to do this without getting rid of individual in-baskets and combining them all? Not to mention, since each associate is a shared resource whose activities take different amounts time to complete, they'd all be waiting around for one another to finish their work. Surely, we don't want to do that!"

Jennifer paused for a moment, appeared to arrange her thoughts, and then said, "Let me reply to your two concerns: shared resources and different or varying task times.

"We talked about shared resources a short time ago, and we can overcome the challenges they present by using part-time continuous flow instead of full-time continuous flow. We can co-locate associates for regularly scheduled periods of time, during which we have them operate in continuous flow, or make-one, move-one fashion. We call this group a *processing cell,* and we set it up to produce at a certain takt capability. When the cell meets, there are no in-baskets, priority changes, or interruptions. Essentially, by creating part-time continuous flow, we're able remove those in-baskets between associates since work is continuously moving and never waiting." She went to the easel and drew a diagram of the idea.

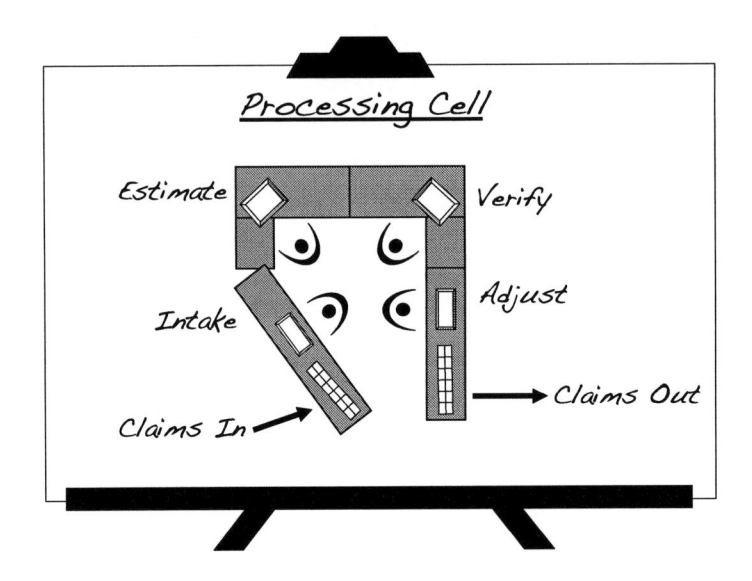

[Figure: Whiteboard sketch titled "Processing Cell" showing a U-shaped cell layout with stations labeled Estimate, Verify, Intake, Adjust, with Claims In entering and Claims Out exiting.]

I nodded to Jennifer and gave her a look of partial satisfaction. I understood the part-time co-location idea, but I still doubted that Jennifer could get all the associates in the cell to do their work in the same amount of time.

Continuing, she said, "Additionally, Pat, for this part-time cell to function properly, we need to make sure everyone's work takes roughly the same amount of time to complete. We don't want anyone in the cell waiting to receive work from the previous person or activity.

"Let me introduce another term called work elements. A work element is defined as the smallest, discrete increment of required work that can be moved to another person. They're logical breaking points in the sequence of tasks we do that make up the work as we know it: thinking, composing, editing, calculating, filing, communicating, documenting, retrieving, saving, etc. We take everyone's discrete tasks that make up the total process, disassociate those tasks from specific individuals, and then redistribute them in sequence so each associate's total work takes slightly less time than the established takt capability time.

"So, we give the first associate in our processing cell enough work elements, in the correct sequence, of course, so that he or she produces at slightly less than the established takt capability time. We then take the remaining work elements and continue to redistribute them in sequence to the next associate in the processing cell until he or she also produces at slightly less than the established takt capability time. We continue until we're out of work elements."

Jennifer sketched this out for us on the flip chart.

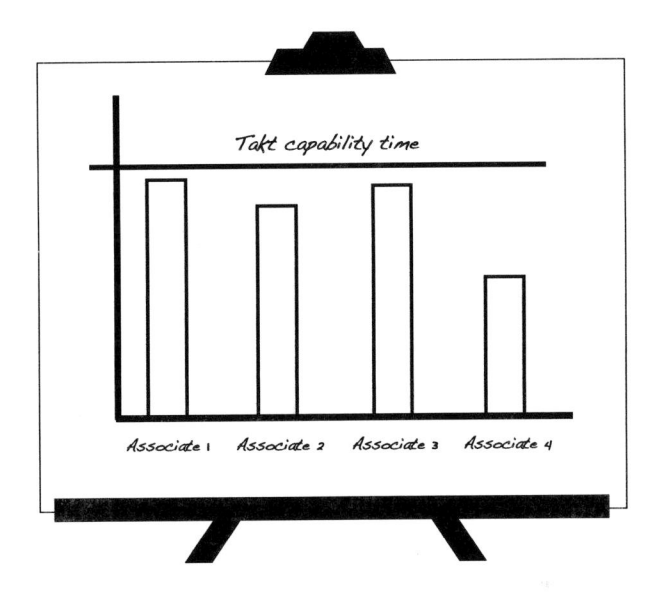

[Flip chart showing a bar graph with a horizontal line labeled "Takt capability time" and four bars labeled "Associate 1", "Associate 2", "Associate 3", "Associate 4"]

She continued, "If the work elements for the last person in the cell fall farther below the takt capability time, that's okay. For everyone else, we want the work elements to add up to slightly less than the takt capability time, or at least as close as possible.

"I've oversimplified things here somewhat. And I recognize that we may bump up against some personal barriers when we do this, but that's a cultural issue. For right now, though, can you see how the work element concept can be used to redistribute work, create and maintain flow, and avoid having people sit around and wait?"

"You've certainly made a good argument for part-time continuous flow, and addressed the issues I had. But I'll have to think about the specifics some more," I admitted. "In the meantime, what do you do with a work element that's tied to a person with a unique skill?"

"Good question, Pat, and it tells me you're actually considering how you might apply this idea at your company," replied Jennifer in a relieved tone. "When we go to implement, we may need to do some cross-training if someone's skill set or knowledge prevents us from achieving continuous flow."

Peyton spoke up next. "It seems like the work elements can be reassigned to accommodate various takt capabilities, but what happens when we actually have to produce to different takt capabilities? It seems like a lot of work to reassign all those work elements every time the takt capability changes."

Jennifer smiled and said, "Another great observation. We'll be talking about something called standard work in guideline number five, which will help us capture and define how we distribute the work elements for each takt capability. When the takt capability changes, the associates might meet more often, work longer hours, or add people to the cell. The standard work tells them what to do in each case, again, without management. The associates simply reference the different, pre-established distributions in work elements. So, to answer your question, the different work element distributions have already been established before they are ever needed or used.

"There are many options for designing your processing cell to meet different takt capabilities. I won't get into the details now – I'll leave those for the reference books[1] – but it's possible to figure out how many associates you need for each takt capability, and the time for which they're needed."

I thought about everything Jennifer had explained and said, "But none of this is really new. I saw something like this at my old company. One of the departments had a study hall period, during which a group of associates would meet each day for a specific, uninterrupted period of time to complete their routine assignments. I'm not sure they took it to the level of takt capability or work element distribution, but the group had a good performance record."

Jennifer responded, "Well, I certainly don't know what happened at

---

[1] See the "Further Reading List" at the back of this book.

your old company, so I can't say what they did or didn't do. But, based on my experience, I know that some companies do a great job creating isolated cells, or something we might call pockets of flow, very similar to what we just discussed. What they usually fail to do, however, is *connect* those isolated cells to all the other activities that have to take place in the office to complete the work.

"They might create good, isolated pockets of flow, but the work just piles up and waits somewhere else in the office because nothing is connected. This is a great segue into our next guideline."

#3: FIFO

Jennifer continued to the next topic without missing a beat. "Now, we may be able to create some part-time continuous flow, but we're going to encounter situations that will prevent us from creating continuous flow everywhere. So, let's talk about what we can do if that happens, since it will likely be the case in our offices.

"If we can't create continuous flow everywhere, we're going to use a guideline called FIFO, which stands for first-in, first-out. Most people are familiar with this term from its use in accounting. For our purposes, though, we want to think of FIFO as a form of flow used to regulate the sequence and volume of work between two disconnected or imbalanced activities. This could be connecting a processing cell to the next activity, or just connecting two activities, neither of which are processing cells.

"Let's do an exercise to help us understand how FIFO works. Say we introduce blue, green, yellow, and red colored ping pong balls into the top end of a pipe. In what order do you think the balls would come out the other end of the pipe?"

"In the same order they went in," replied Peyton. "Blue, green, yellow, and red. That's a no brainer."

"Good," said Jennifer. "Now, let's imagine that Pat is loading the pipe with a certain colored ping pong ball, and Peyton is unloading a ball from the pipe at a regular time interval. Pat, you have a large supply of colored ping pong balls, but let's say the pipe is only long enough to hold eight at a time. What's the lowest and highest number of ping pong balls that could be in the pipe at any given time?"

"Zero and eight," replied Peyton.

"Right," said Jennifer. "Do you see how the length of the pipe controlled the amount of ping pong balls that could go into it? It's very different from an in-basket, where files stack up higher than the sides, and any number of jobs might be present.

"In our exercise, Peyton, you were removing individual ping pong balls from the pipe, but how did you decide which ping pong ball to take when you were ready for the next one?"

Peyton seemed a bit puzzled, then replied, "I'm not sure what you're getting at. I wouldn't really have any choice. I would just take whichever ping pong ball is next in line in the pipe. It's not like I could pull some out until I found a favorite color and then reload the extras back into the pipe, could I?"

Jennifer smiled and said, "Perhaps it was an ambiguous question, but I like your answer. You're right, you would simply withdraw the next one from the pipe."

Jennifer then went to the flip chart and constructed a diagram of two activities named Pat and Peyton, and connected them with two parallel lines. Underneath the lines, she wrote "FIFO," and on top of them, she wrote "Max = 5 Balls." Then, she proceeded to add balls of various colors.

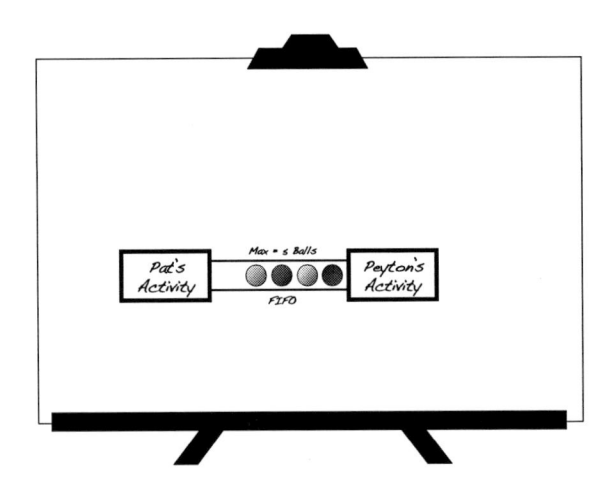

"This diagram represents how we would connect two processes together using a FIFO lane," she said. "You'll see something like this when we take our tour this afternoon, but with jobs, or work, not balls." When she finished drawing, Jennifer turned to us and asked, "When the FIFO lane fills up, what happens to each of your activities?"

I commented, "Well, I wouldn't be able to put any more balls into the pipe. I'd have nothing to do."

"If you're a shared resource," replied Jennifer, "you'd likely do something else for a while until an empty spot opens up in the FIFO lane. You're correct, however, in assuming that if you continue to process work meant for Peyton's process, it would have nowhere to go. That would be a problem."

Peyton said, "I don't see any difference for me. I would just keep doing what I normally do, but I imagine I'd be able to see when the FIFO lane becomes full, right?"

"That's right, replied Jennifer, "and we're going to talk more about what we do in that situation when we get to the second part of our definition of Operational Excellence about fixing flow before it breaks down."

Jennifer turned back to the diagram and added another FIFO lane off to Peyton's right and connected it to a processing cell. It was clear from the example that the processing cell would always know what to work on next from the FIFO lane that fed it.

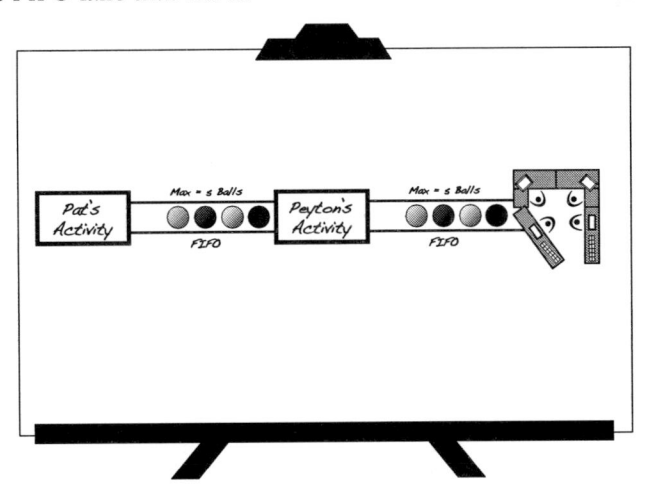

"For the moment, though, I want you to recall the five questions we asked earlier to determine if we had flow," said Jennifer. "Peyton, do you want to try answering them again, this time using this example? And let's say it takes you twenty minutes to 'process' a ball from the FIFO lane once you withdraw it."

"Okay," said Peyton. "I'll give it a try. The first question is 'How do I know what to work on next?' That's easy. I just take whatever is in the FIFO lane. The second question is 'Where do I get my work from?' That one's simple, too. I get it from the FIFO lane, and I'm sure in a real one, there would be a specific spot from which I would retrieve my work. The third question is 'How long should it take to perform my work?' Jennifer, you said twenty minutes.

"The fourth question is 'Where do I send my work once I'm finished with it?' I would put it in the FIFO lane that feeds Jennifer's activity. Again, in a real-life setting, I'm sure there would be a specific spot in which I'd put completed work. The fifth question is 'When do I send my work once I'm finished with it?' Jennifer's FIFO lane controls this one. I'd have to wait until a space opens up in that lane, and that's where my work would go when I'm finished with it."

"Nicely done," said Jennifer.

"That's why FIFO is considered a form of flow, isn't it?" I asked. "Because we're able to answer those five questions?"

"Exactly," said Jennifer. "And that brings us to the next guideline."

#4: Work-Flow Cycles

"A *work-flow* cycle refers to the rate at which work moves or flows within or between different work areas or activities along a specific pathway. This guideline builds on what we already established with our other ones," Jennifer advised. "And it adds structure and discipline to them, too.

"Work-flow cycles help us stabilize and regulate flow in the office, and they enable everyone to know the time at which they're going to receive their work. It's not an expediting system, but rather an indicator that tells us when work is going to flow along preset pathways. To ensure consistent, predictable results, work-flow cycles should occur at preset time intervals.

"Let me give you a specific example," said Jennifer, as she walked back to the easel. "In our FIFO exercise, let's look at the processing cell. We would define a work-flow cycle that describes the time at which the cell will process jobs. We might design it so the cell processes and flows work every day for two hours, beginning at one o'clock." Jennifer drew on the flip chart, adding more information to the previous FIFO example.

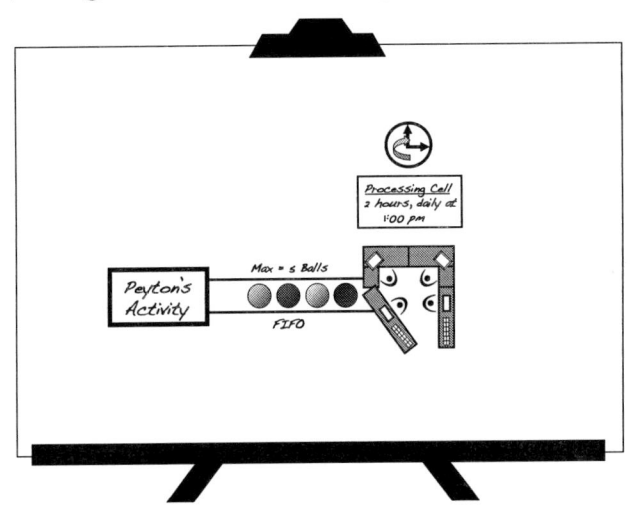

She continued, "We want to create a work-flow cycle at this level whether we're dealing with an activity done by only one associate or a processing cell staffed with multiple associates. Somewhere in the area, we want to indicate to everyone working in the office that the associates in the cell have essentially promised to process everything in the FIFO lane by a certain time each day."

"So, this helps the associates know when to expect output from a particular activity or processing cell?" I asked.

"Yes," said Jennifer. "Because work flows at the processing cell at a preset time and along a preset pathway, everyone knows when they should expect to get their work from it. But that's not all. The work-flow cycle concept applies between activities and processing cells, too. Not only do we want each individual office activity or processing cell to have an established work-flow cycle, we also want the connections between them to have work-flow cycles. If everything in the office operates to a work-flow cycle, then we're able to establish a *guaranteed turnaround time* for the entire office." She added even more detail to the example.

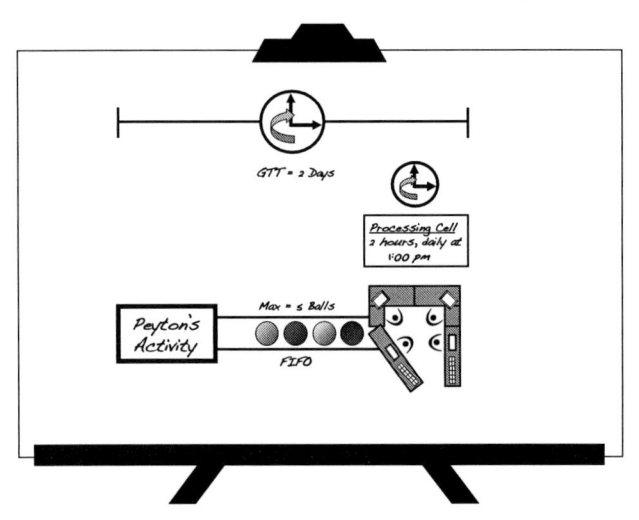

[Figure: Whiteboard diagram showing GTT = 2 Days, Processing Cell 2 hours, daily at 1:00 pm, Peyton's Activity, Max = 5 Balls, FIFO]

"We can do this because we know long it takes for work to be completed at each individual step, and we also know when work will be passed along to the next activity through the FIFO lane. If we know these two elements at every step in our office, then we know the guaranteed turnaround time for the entire office. Think of the advantage you would have over your competitors if you could provide guaranteed turnaround times to your customers."

"It makes sense," said Peyton. "No wonder this system is being introduced to other areas here. It not only creates flow, but it establishes guaranteed turnaround times for our work that we can share with our customers."

"You got it," said Jennifer. "And having work-flow cycles eliminates the need for countless voicemails and emails, since people know when they'll receive their information. Each area in the office knows when a claim will be finished, so they don't need to check on it."

"The work-flow cycle concept isn't as confusing as I first thought," I commented. "So, this is mostly about having standardized procedures for the flow, right?"

Jennifer smiled and said, "I think you're hinting at standard work, Pat. Let's talk about that now. It's the next guideline. We need to develop robust standard work to establish regularity and consistency in our activities, continuous flow processing cells, and FIFO lanes. When we do, we'll hit our work-flow cycles and guaranteed turnaround times every time."

#5: Standard Work for Flow

Jennifer said, "The fifth guideline is critical to the successful operation of our office. Standard work means establishing the one best way to do a job or task, and then ensuring everyone uses that method so that the work required is performed in a consistent amount of time. Standard work helps us create a disciplined plan that all associates can follow. And we won't just have standard work for how we do things in the office, we'll also have standard work for the flow.

"In our office, we need to develop standard work for the flow of intellectual property, and flow cannot exist without stability and repeatability in the things we do. Continuous flow, FIFO, and work-flow cycles provide the pathway and timing for flow, and standard work helps make the pathways and connections robust and keeps work moving along the connections we set up.

"It's not always easy to create or sustain standard work in the office. Education and leadership are critical, and so is a destination so people understand exactly what standard work should look like once it's achieved. Management needs to prepare the organization first and then drive the process and methodology for creating standard work.

"Is there a go-to person in your office who knows how to get things done? In most organizations, a lot of activities happen only because of the longevity of the work force, or something we call tribal knowledge. Different individuals informally create work standards that they use to complete their work correctly. But, the details generally aren't documented, and the knowledge resides only with a few people, which means it has the potential to be discarded when people take vacation, are relocated, or retire.

"Standard work captures the best practices and lessons learned from each associate. Having the work defined and documented makes training more effective for new or temporary employees. A consistent approach and methodology also minimizes the chance of introducing noise or chaos into the system. Things are done correctly, consistently, and with less variation from person to person since everyone uses the same method. In essence, standard work leads to better quality, lower cost, and improved morale."

I got the feeling Jennifer had lots of experience discussing this topic. She seemed to speak with authority, wisdom, and as someone who had fought this battle many times before.

She continued, "People learn in three different ways: by hearing, seeing, and doing. We retain less than five percent of the information we hear when we we're learning something new. When we see it, we retain about sixty percent. But, when we learn by doing, we retain approximately ninety percent of the information, because we trust what we do. Standard work makes use of the best methods of learning by allowing associates to participate in the learning. They hear it explained, watch the process, and then perform the task using standard work to guide them. What method have we been using this morning?"

Peyton spoke up. "Mostly hearing. There's been a little seeing, because of your drawings, but I guess we can't be expected to remember much by tomorrow."

That frightened me. I'd heard a lot of good stuff so far, and to think I might not be able to put it all together for Chris was very disturbing.

Jennifer replied, "That's right, and that's why we're rushing through this morning. Before the memories fade, I want you to take the tour and see what you've heard. Peyton, you'll have the opportunity to actually *do* all of this in the near future. Pat, hopefully the sixty percent retention rate will work for you if you lean on your experience.

"Alright, back to standard work. Once we develop standard work, we should always use it since it represents the best method for how to do things. If you stop and think about it, why would we ever use anything else?

"Once we create standard work, we need to recognize that it can be improved at any time. However, it's difficult to improve results if we only rely on one person or a select few, especially if one of them is the boss. If you're looking for ways to improve existing standard work, make sure you involve everyone."

Shifting gears, Jennifer suggested we jot down the next part. "In Operational Excellence, there are three distinct levels of standard work. At each level, standard work is an actionable document that everyone can see and share. Standard work is not simple to create, but knowing what level of standard work is required makes creating it more efficient and applicable. Be sure to keep the levels separate rather than trying to combine all three into one standard work document."

Jennifer started on a new page on the flip chart and wrote down the three levels.

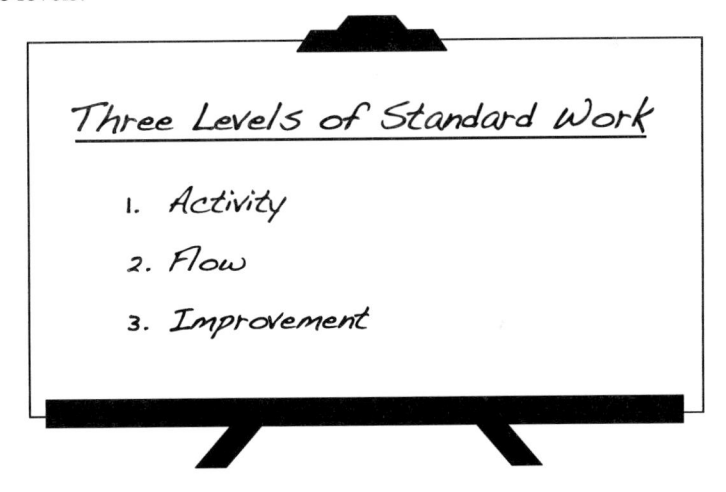

> **Three Levels of Standard Work**
> 1. Activity
> 2. Flow
> 3. Improvement

She continued, "Each of these represents a level at which we need standard work. I'll explain each level and what the differences are between them.

"Activity level standard work occurs at the level of an individual. Here, we want to describe what the job is, who is responsible for doing it (titles, not people's names), and how long they should work on it. This makes for a better and more optimized process. Any questions about activity level standard work?"

I felt an obligation to ask, given the opportunity. "So, activity level standard work just details what an associate does for the job, things like the file used, the references, the specifics about documenting or creating a claim entry," I said. "This is where I might use photos, diagrams, screen shots…stuff like that, right?"

Jennifer replied, "That's correct. It doesn't need to be complicated. In fact, the simpler the better. Also, remember that whatever you create will likely be improved regularly, so structure your documentation to allow for that and, as a leader, encourage it.

"Let's look at the flow level next. This is where we connect the activity of one person to the activity of another. This level of standard work answers questions like: how do I know what to work on next? How and when do I pass work to the next process? What are the connections between activities? These are all flow level questions, and they involve team activities and multiple people. Any questions here?"

Peyton spoke up, "So, this is where the rules for work-flow cycles, FIFO, and takt capability would come into play?"

Jennifer responded, "Yes, exactly, and it's also where our five questions for business process flow come into play. If we have good flow level standard work, then we should be able to answer all five questions for each connection in our office." Jennifer flipped back to the easel page with the five questions for business process flow.

Five Questions for Business Process Flow

1. How do I know what to work on next?
2. Where do I get my work from?
3. How long should it take me to perform my work?
4. Where do I send my work once I'm finished with it?
5. When do I send my work once I'm finished with it?

She continued, "Flow level standard work establishes the standard of normal flow between activities. If employees can see normal flow, then they can see abnormal flow, which I'll talk more about later.

"The last level of standard work is improvement. This level documents and standardizes how new ideas are deployed to the team. It encourages the individuals working with the process to make suggestions, and establishes how to assess those suggestions. This might sound kind of funny, but you should have standard work to manage any changes to your standard work. You don't want to unintentionally limit your improvement opportunities."

With the morning slipping away, and apparently much more to cover, Jennifer's pace picked up noticeably. "You see," she continued, "all of these guidelines tie together, and it's difficult to separate them when they build on one another in an integrated system. The first five guidelines we covered – takt time, or takt capability, continuous flow, FIFO, work-flow cycles, and standard work – all make up how we design our flow. The next three guidelines we're going to cover describe how we actually operate it on a day-to-day basis.

"Let's take a short break and have lunch. We'll be ordering from the deli in our cafeteria, so here's a menu for each of you. Just check off what you want and it'll be delivered so we can continue our conversation while we eat. Sorry to take that hour away from you, but we're packing a lot into one day."

Jennifer collected our forms and handed them to someone who was responsible for making sure our orders got to the right place at the right time. While we waited for our lunches, I reviewed my notes, and was eager to see what would come next.

Chapter 7

The Education, Part II

After the break, Jennifer pulled us together for a quick review before moving on.

"Let's do a recap of the first five guidelines," said Jennifer. "Who wants to tell me what they are?"

"The first guideline is takt time, or takt capability," I said, "and it's dependent on demand, demand variation, and shared resources. If we have these variables, and we pretty much always do in the office, then we need to establish preset takt capabilities to cover the varying ranges of demand."

Peyton jumped in and said, "The second guideline is continuous flow, where we analyze all the activities, co-locate associates, balance work elements, and design a part-time cell that operates on a make-one, move-one basis. Because we set up this cell with the ability to flex to different takt capabilities as well as meet at regular, preset times, we always know when information will flow.

"The third guideline is FIFO, which is a form of flow used to regulate the sequence and volume of work between two disconnected or imbalanced activities. FIFO allows us to keep work in sequence between activities if we're not using continuous flow. It also creates robust connections between activities in the office."

"The fourth guideline is work-flow cycles," I offered, "which we use to establish preset pathways and times for the flow of information between activities and connections throughout the entire office. With robust work-flow cycles, we're able to flow work through our office at guaranteed turnaround times.

"The fifth guideline is standard work, which helps establish regularity and consistency at our activities, continuous flow processing cells, and FIFO lanes. Standard work is applied at the activity level to tell us how a process should function, at the flow level to link different activities, and at the improvement level to update the standard work system. Standard work enables us to consistently hit our work-flow cycles and predictably flow work through the office."

"Wow," said Jennifer. "You both pass with flying colors."

"So, are we done now?" I asked.

"Not yet," said Jennifer. "Remember, the first five guidelines were all about how we design our office for flow. The remaining ones we're going to cover are about how we actually operate that flow. Let's get started on the last three."

#6: Single Point Initialization

Jennifer continued, "Now, we want to address how we initialize work into the flow. When an assignment is started in a typical business process, each associate sets his or her own priorities and then pushes their completed work to the next step, whether it needs it or is ready for it. This approach provides no regularity or predictability to the flow of work in the office, and it causes us to meddle and shift priorities around.

"Using the first five guidelines, we've designed an office where each activity is linked or connected in flow all the way to the customer." Jennifer walked to the easel and added a person to the diagram she had drawn earlier.

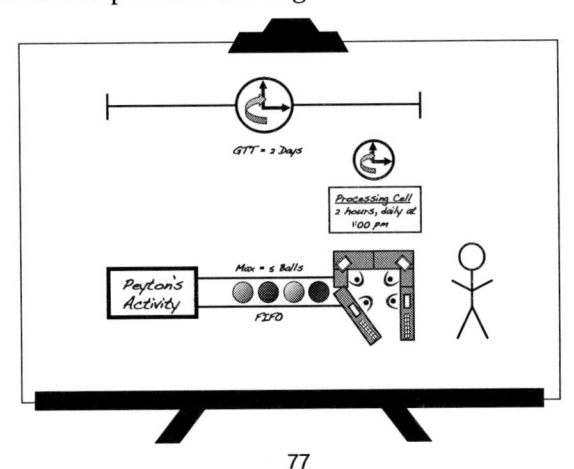

"Here's our customer all the way on the right," she continued, pointing at the stick figure. "And on the left are the activities and connections that deliver our work to that customer. But where and how does the work get started? We want to have only one place at which we initialize the flow, and we call this our single point of initialization.

"All of our office flow happens *after* the point at which we initialize the work. From there, we process in continuous flow or FIFO all the way to the customer. This is an important point because if the sequence of work remains fixed after the single point of initialization, and if we know how long each step takes, then we can predict the time it'll take for work to be completed once it's been released into our system. That's how we're able to create and live by those guaranteed turnaround times we've been talking about."

Peyton reiterated what we had heard, "So, we introduce a job at the single point of initialization and, after that, we have flow all the way to the customer so the sequence of work remains fixed. Doing this creates a guaranteed turnaround time for the entire flow and allows us to predict the time by which we'll complete the work. And, just to be clear, you're talking about the same work that's in my department right now, all those jobs that have unknown completion dates?"

"Yep! That's pretty much it," replied Jennifer with a smile. "Sound believable?"

"Not really," I replied. "I admit you've constructed a good case for designing flow to improve performance, but you're telling us that we can launch a job into the office, never change priorities, and be certain of its completion time! I've got to see it to believe it."

"Well, later today, you'll get to see it happen," replied Jennifer. "I remember how astonished I was when I saw it in action the first time. The tour this afternoon should be like a walk through an amusement park for you. But right now, I want to make sure the concept at least makes sense."

"It does," I said. "I'm just not sure how to make it happen."

"Fair enough," said Jennifer. "Let's get back to our discussion so we'll have time for the tour. In our diagram, is there one point at which we could initialize the work that would enable every other activity to know what to do next?"

Jennifer waited for a response. Not getting one, she continued, "Let's look to the left of the customer. We have a processing cell operating on a work-flow cycle of two hours each day. The jobs come to it from the FIFO lane and are then processed. The processing cell always knows what to do next because the FIFO lane maintains the sequence of work that comes from Peyton's activity." Jennifer drew a circle around Peyton's activity.

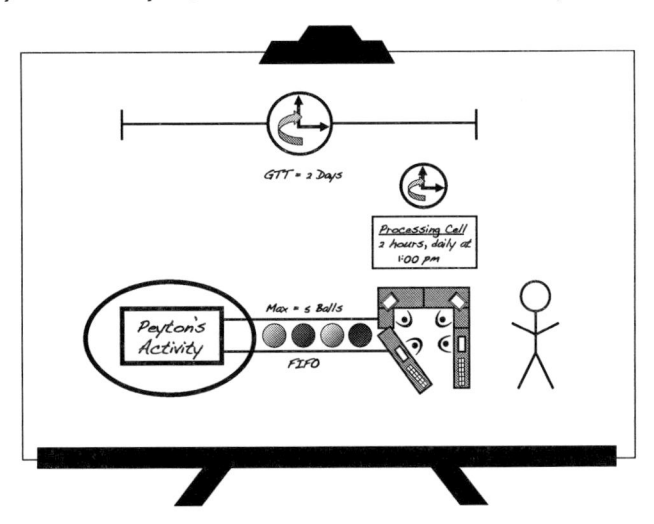

She continued, "Peyton's activity is the only one that needs to be scheduled since the processing cell will know what to work on next based on what comes to it in the FIFO lane."

Jennifer pointed at Peyton's activity and said, "This is the first activity. How does Peyton know what to do? Well, Peyton's work comes in from the customer. In this example, the customer requests a ball, so Peyton processes the ball and then puts it into the FIFO lane. After that, we have either continuous flow or FIFO all the way to the customer, so the sequence of work never changes.

"The reason we aim for door-to-door flow in our business processes is so the work comes out in the same order it goes in. Once we introduce work at the single point of initialization, the sequence never changes, and this establishes a guaranteed turnaround time for the entire office.

"It's important to become aware of problems at the single point of initialization because this is where the work is structured and sequenced for every other activity and processing cell in the office. If we have issues there, then we'll end up with irregular flow, and that's when managers tend to want to jump in."

A question popped into my mind. "It seems that our single point of initialization might have a bit of uncertainty around it if we need to follow up on certain customer requests or clarify information, stuff like that. Also, priorities might get shifted at that point before work gets released into the flow. Is that accurate?"

"Yes," answered Jennifer, "but this is the only place where we anticipate anything like that happening. If a customer request isn't sufficiently complete to process when we receive it, unfortunately, we can't release it into the flow. We have to clarify information or request missing data, and we need to develop standard work to do it. But, even though there might be some uncertainty at the single point of initialization, after that, we've essentially eliminated the chaos that used to exist since it all takes place up front. Does that answer your question?"

"Yes," I said. "It's a lot to digest, but I understand the concepts."

"Also," continued Jennifer, "keep in mind that while we've moved all the clarification up front, it's still a waste of time, and if we can minimize it, then we can minimize the need for prioritization. But, removing all the uncertainty and reprioritization from the activities that come *after* the single point of initialization is what allows us to establish a guaranteed turnaround time for the office.

"If we start a sequence of jobs at the single point of initialization and have flow all the way after it, would there ever be a need for prioritization? Why or why not?"

Peyton spoke up, "Once a job is in flow, we don't need to shuffle anything around since the desired sequence of work has already been established at the single point of initialization and is preserved all the way to the customer. And, since every job has a guaranteed turnaround time associated with it, we'll always know when a job should be complete. Each job is already being done as quickly as possible, so why would we want to interfere with that?

"If something happened, instead of changing priorities, I'd probably just check to make sure we were using the correct takt capability and verify that our standard work is correct. It seems like it would make more sense to critique the system rather than expedite a specific job, which would ignore the underlying problem."

I jumped in and asked, "But what happens when the information on a claim finally comes through and now it's a rush because it's so far behind? Surely we're not just going to let it wait in line behind all the others."

"Unexpected things will always happen," said Jennifer. "We can't predict everything. But we're always going to try and let the system handle anything that comes up because it's designed to be flexible. For example, if a claim is in rush status, we could run our work-flow cycles for longer than normal, or perhaps start them a few hours earlier. The point is that we're going to look to *the system* when something unexpected happens and *not* to the decisions of managers.

"I think we're ready to shift gears. Until now, we've been talking about the first part of the definition of Operational Excellence. Who can remind me what that is?"

I spoke up and said, "Where we see the flow of value to the customer."

"That's right," said Jennifer, "and everything we've covered has been necessary for us to see the flow of value to the customer. But let me ask you: why are we creating flow in the first place? What's so good about flow?"

Peyton and I sat quietly for a few minutes before I answered. "Because creating flow is the best way to eliminate waste." I was confident in my answer, but I got the sense that Jennifer was after something much deeper.

"This is a tricky one," she said. "Although it's true that creating flow is the best way to eliminate waste, the real reason we create flow is simply *so we can see when flow stops*. If flow has stopped, then we know something has gone wrong, and we can step in, fix it, and get the flow back on track. Actually, you and I won't step in. The employees will.

"This gets us into the second part of the definition of Operational Excellence, fixing flow before it breaks down. The next two guidelines explain how to create a system that lets us know if things are going right or wrong, and how we can set up our employees to fix flow before it breaks down."

#7: Visual Indicators

"Next, we'll look at something called visual indicators, which are used for two purposes. First, they let the people in the flow see if things are going right or starting to go wrong, and second, they enable everyone else to know if information will get to the next activity, processing cell, or FIFO lane on time.

"Now that we understand the way knowledge and information flows in our office and how and why it gets initiated at only one point, let's talk about how we can see if things are going right or wrong, and how often we should do so. Do you think we can see how well things are going in today's offices?"

"Is that a rhetorical question?" asked Peyton. "Because the answer is, not really. Any checks by management happen in meetings or are totally random, kind of like a surprise audit. But, in their defense, they have no way of knowing if everyone is completing their jobs on time unless they stand over their shoulders and watch them work."

"And sometimes, that kind of micromanagement is what drives changes in priorities," I added. "That, and not knowing when the work will be completed."

Jennifer knew she struck a chord with her question. "Your responses are spot on," she said. "Let's think about how often we should know if our system is keeping up with customer demand. Should a manager know every Friday, so he or she can prepare an end-of-week report? Probably not, because if customer demand has changed during the week or things have fallen behind somewhere, then there wouldn't be enough time left to do anything about it."

Peyton and I nodded in agreement. "I'd want to know there's a problem as soon as one arises," I said.

"Fair enough," said Jennifer. "But how would you actually go about doing this? Would you walk through the office every hour to see what's on time and what's behind by asking each associate how it's going? If you took this approach, how much time would you spend at your desk getting your own work done? And what signs would you look for when strolling around that would tip you off to a problem?"

"I'm not sure," I said, "but I'd know a problem if I saw one. Though, I probably *would* spend a lot of time asking questions and fixing things."

"You're exactly right," said Jennifer. "But I don't want *you* fixing anything. We want to have visual indicators that tell everyone when things are going right or starting to go wrong. We also want to establish a predetermined time at which we know our system is keeping up with the rate of customer demand. Visual indicators give everyone a true sense of the pulse of the office and also a feeling of accomplishment."

Jennifer checked to see that we were still attentive, then continued. "A good visual indicator would be moving work from one activity or processing cell at a preset time and delivering it to the next process in the flow. Either the work moved at the preset time or it didn't. And if it didn't, then something is wrong.

"To be clear, this is not about how often a manager or supervisor checks on the associates working in their area. Rather, it's about how often the associates know whether or not the flow is working the way it's supposed to. Our visual indicators measure the *system*, not the people operating it."

Jennifer gave us time to grasp what she said, then continued. "Visual indicators are not always easy to create. However, they should have three important attributes. They should be visual, physical, and binary." She went over to the easel and wrote them down.

> **Three Attributes of Visual Indicators**
> 1. Visual
> 2. Physical
> 3. Binary

Jennifer continued, "Let me explain a bit more. By visual, I mean we should be able to see whether we're on time without asking anyone. By physical, I mean some activity must happen, like a file is moved, a tray is emptied, etc. The best physical activity is actually moving work from one process to the next. By binary, I mean the flow happened or it did not.

"So, how often should we know if the system is meeting customer demand?"

"I don't have a clue," I smiled and said, "but I'm sure you'll be able to clear it up."

Jennifer responded, "Thanks for your confidence. Like we agreed before, knowing at the end of every week is too infrequent. How about the other end of the spectrum? Imagine if our office processes worked really fast, let's say three minutes per job. Would we want to know every three minutes if the system was working?"

"No way!" I said.

"Why not?" pressed Jennifer.

"Because if something went wrong, there wouldn't be enough time to do anything about it," I said. "There's no way anyone could react and fix things inside a three-minute window. Plus, my associates would get sick of me if I wanted to know about their progress every three minutes."

"Very good," said Jennifer. "Depending on what you do in your office and how long your jobs take, the time increment used can vary. Generally, though, a good time increment for a visual indicator is at the end of a work-flow cycle." Jennifer went to the easel and added more detail to her previous example.

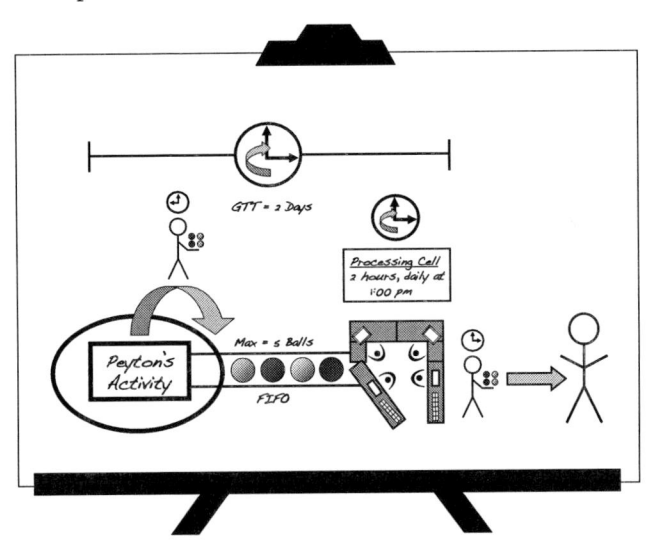

She continued, "The figure carrying the balls would be the person moving information to the next processing cell, activity, or even FIFO lane. Don't worry about the number of balls. In real life, this person would move the amount of work that was completed at the end of each work-flow cycle. The clock above him means this happens at preset times. Just like the illustration, this can and probably will happen at different times for different processes.

"Don't worry if you miss your time target in the beginning. In fact, you likely will until the associates get comfortable with the new way of doing things. Remember, though, that the visual indicators are a check on the system, not the people operating it. Make sure your people understand this, otherwise it can be pretty discouraging if the time target is missed. Notice that I didn't say 'when the *associates* miss the time target.' The success of the visual indicators depends not only on how you deal with the technicalities involved, but on how you introduce it to your people and how they understand it.

"What really counts, though, is what the people in the flow do when they see it's starting to break down, because that means something has gone wrong and needs to be fixed. What we do about it and how we handle it brings us to our next and last guideline."

At that point, our lunches arrived, so we took a few minutes to get the food unwrapped and agreed to continue our discussion as we ate.

#8: Changes In Customer Demand

"We've gone through seven guidelines so far," said Jennifer. "We've established multiple takt capabilities, continuous flow, FIFO, work-flow cycles, standard work, a single point of initialization, and visual indicators. We've even been able to set up a guaranteed turnaround time for the entire flow through the office. What more could we need?" Jennifer paused, expecting Peyton and I to pick up the conversation from there.

Peyton took the hint and gave Jennifer a chance to get started on her lunch. "Well, what about if we end up routinely maxing out or exceeding our takt capability? Or, what do we do when the flow starts to break down?"

I heard what Peyton said, and then it hit me. "Great point, Peyton, but how exactly would we *know* we're exceeding our takt capability? How would we know the flow has started to break down? Are you going to explain that, Jennifer?"

"I sure am," said Jennifer, taking a bite of her salad before continuing. "Our eighth guideline is something called changes in customer demand or, perhaps better put, *reacting* to changes in customer demand. It's going to really get into the second part of the definition of Operational Excellence, where we fix flow before it breaks down.

"First, we need to be able to react to the normal variation we experience on a day-to-day basis. Next, we have to recognize when the actual demand has increased, which is something we expect to happen as we strive for Operational Excellence. As we begin to regularly meet or exceed our customers' expectations, it's possible – and even likely – that they'll reward us with more business, especially if we can outperform the competition.

Operational Excellence is a foundation for business growth, and if we achieve it, our business will grow. But more on that later.

"Right now, we want to address how we recognize and respond to changing customer demand. First, we need to understand what we normally deal with to know whether it's becoming or has become abnormal. Let's look at this graph." Jennifer handed us a sheet of paper.

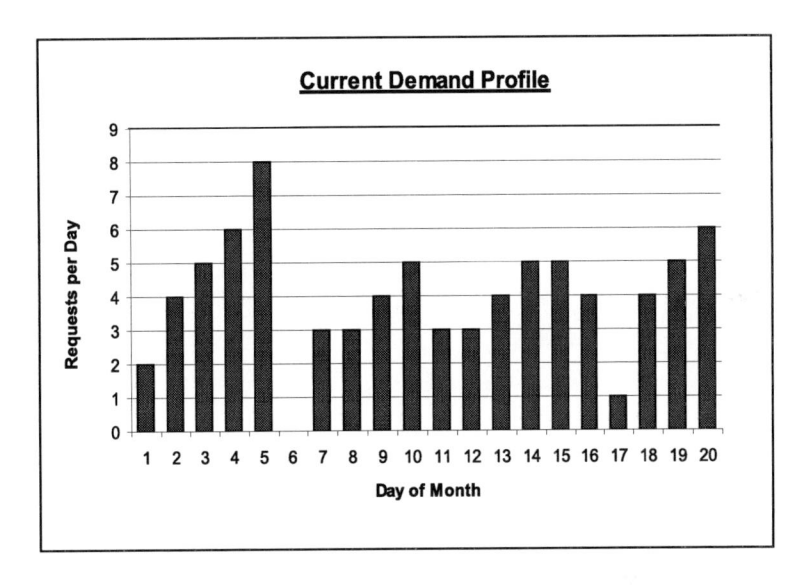

Current Demand Profile

[Bar chart showing Requests per Day for Days 1-20 of the month: Day 1: 2, Day 2: 4, Day 3: 5, Day 4: 6, Day 5: 8, Day 6: 0, Day 7: 3, Day 8: 3, Day 9: 4, Day 10: 5, Day 11: 3, Day 12: 3, Day 13: 4, Day 14: 5, Day 15: 5, Day 16: 4, Day 17: 1, Day 18: 4, Day 19: 5, Day 20: 6]

"It's important that we start with data," she continued with a smile, "because a person without data is just another person with an opinion. This is the actual demand we experienced four months ago. Note that the biggest demand days are every fifth day, or every Friday. As I mentioned earlier, we determined that some of these peaks were self-imposed because one of our customer service associates was clearing his desk of any procrastinated work at the end of each week. This variation caused the demand to hit us in abnormal and irregular waves, and it was totally unpredictable.

"We were able to eliminate this internally-caused variation but, as you can see from the graph, we still had variation that we couldn't get rid of. So, what do we do? How do we staff for something like this when we have persistent variation?"

"No clue," I said. "I have this problem all the time, and I don't handle it very well."

After a short pause, Jennifer said, "Let me help you out. Earlier, when we were talking about takt capabilities, I mentioned that we need to establish multiple takt capabilities to account for specific ranges of customer demand. What I didn't say at the time is how we should establish our first or normal takt capability, the one we set ourselves up to use on a daily basis.

"We want to set it up to handle roughly eighty percent of the demand variation, and we design our processing cells, FIFO lanes, and work-flow cycles around this. Then, we create different takt capabilities to handle the different ranges in demand we expect to experience over the course of time."

Jennifer went to the easel and drew something that looked like a timecard rack. She added folders in each slot and indicated that the slots would be colored differently.

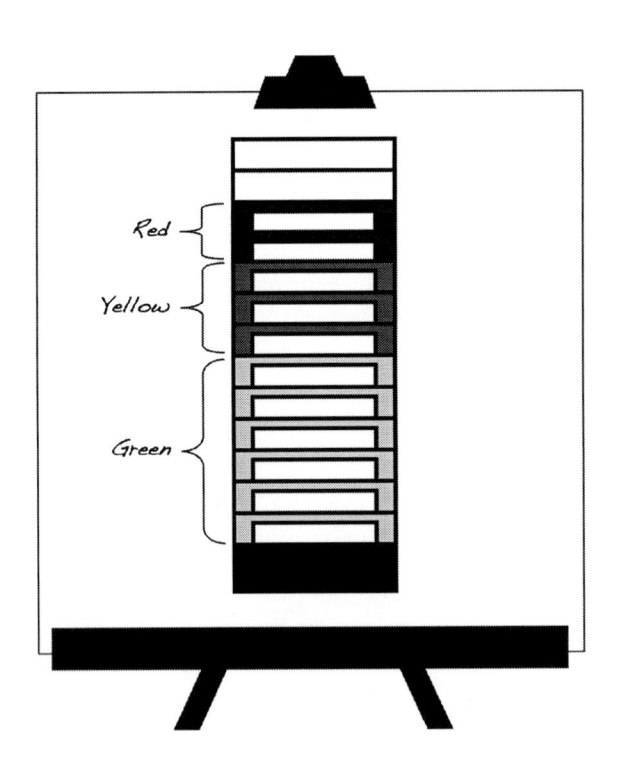

"Each color represents a different takt capability and visually tells the team which one they need to use for that day. The green slots are for the normal takt capability and its associated work-flow cycle. If jobs do not exceed the green portion, then the associates in the cell know they'll be fine operating at their normal takt capability.

"If jobs spill over into the yellow slots, then the associates in the cell know they need to shift to their second takt capability and its associated work-flow cycle to meet the greater demand. Jobs in the red slots mean the associates need to shift to their third takt capability and its associated work-flow cycle. All of this has been pre-established so it's ready to go before the associates even set foot in the cell."

"Okay," said Peyton, "so we know how we're going to handle daily changes in demand, but what happens when the customer dumps another job on us and we exceed the red zone?"

Jennifer added some more detail to the example and labeled the top two slots "Plan B."

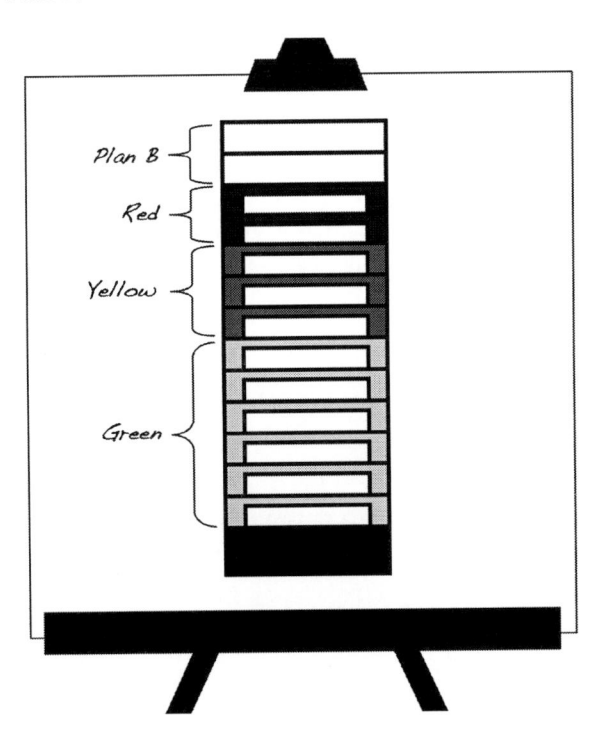

"That can happen," said Jennifer, "and we must pre-establish a Plan B, or standard work, for when demand exceeds our greatest takt capability so it can be automatically deployed when needed. When jobs fall into the slot or slots for Plan B, everyone would know what to do, *without a meeting*.

"The details of standard work for Plan B could encompass any number of different options. We might work longer hours, run the work-flow cycle more often, temporarily add associates, or do something else entirely. The response can vary. It doesn't have to be universal, but it does have to be pre-established.

"Having standard work for different situations gets to the heart of the second part of the definition of Operational Excellence: fixing flow before it breaks down. With this methodology in place, the associates can see flow breaking down. They know immediately if they exceed their maximum takt capability, and their standard work tells them what to do to get back on track. And, in case you haven't guessed by now, this all happens without management intervention of any kind.

"Think of what would happen if we didn't have standard work for when things go wrong. Typically, managers would get involved and change priorities, authorize overtime, or maybe just allow the jobs to be late. They'd make decisions, and *decisions kill flow*. But no more. Now, the associates can see that conditions are becoming abnormal, react to those signals, and fix the flow before it breaks down."

"So," I said, "the system flexes to accommodate the daily variation we experience, and can even signal when we need to tap into our standard work for when things go wrong. And the associates, not managers, are able to react to these changes and fix the flow before it breaks down. But how can we use a system like this to identify not just daily variation, but an overall change in demand that might be more permanent?"

Jennifer said, "We'd want to know if our system is routinely operating in an abnormal state, right? We don't want to live in Plan B all the time, since it most likely represents a sub-optimal way of doing business." Jennifer drew again on the easel while Peyton and I watched.

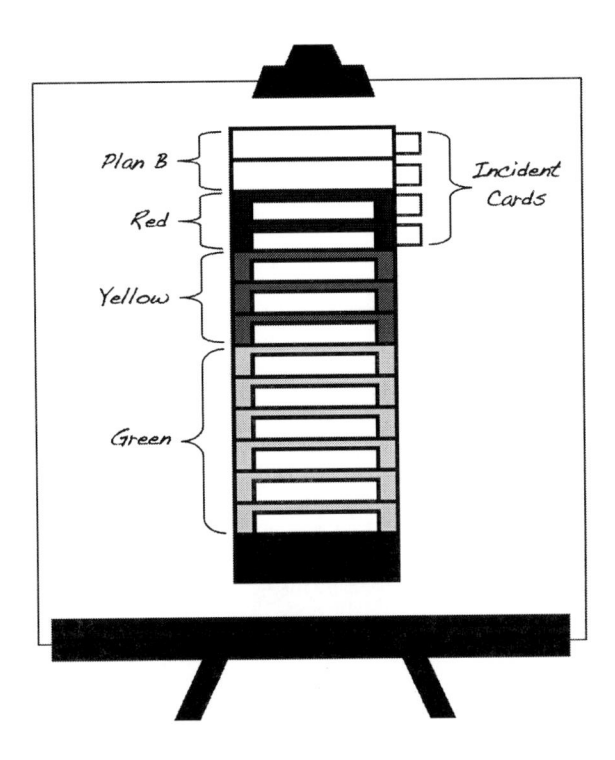

[Figure: Easel displaying a stack of cards labeled from top to bottom — Plan B, Red, Yellow, Green — with a bracket on the right labeling them "Incident Cards".]

She said, "In this example, we would have cards that live in our red and Plan B slots. Each time a job occupies one of these slots, we would remove the card and document the incident. Over time, the frequency with which we hit these slots and mark these cards indicate whether we need to reevaluate our demand profile. In other words, we have an actual *system* for determining whether we need to make changes. We don't just use someone's personal opinion."

"If we're repeatedly tapping into the red or Plan B slots, then what do we do?" I asked.

Jennifer smiled and said, "We celebrate, because it means business is good. Seriously, though, if we recognize that our overall demand profile has increased, then we need to revisit things. We apply the eight guidelines all over again. And yes, I mean *all* eight guidelines, from takt time or takt capability all the way to changes in customer demand, complete with standard work and everything else in between."

Peyton and I sat there, stunned. "Wait, so we just end up repeating the process?" I asked in disbelief.

"You got it," Jennifer said with a smile. "Do you think we should try something *else*? This is the process we used to grow our business, and when our business grows, we simply do it again."

I tried to wrestle with the logic Jennifer threw my way, but to no avail. It made sense. If the eight guidelines for business process flow got us to a point where we'd grown more than we had in the past, then why would we use another process to redesign everything?

"Alright, gang," said Jennifer, "before we go on the tour, keep in mind that I haven't told you everything today. There are more concepts that help us in the office, things like *integration events* that move large chunks of information through different parts of the company. These only happen once a month or so, which is why I didn't cover them.

"There are also *knowledge shares*[sm], which have virtually eliminated all meetings for us. By meetings, I mean when we bring people together and then try to influence, cajole, and arm-twist to make decisions. Perhaps we can talk about knowledge shares and integration events the next time you come visit us.

"If there are no questions, we're going to go on that tour I've been promising. While we're in the office and meeting with the team, feel free to ask questions. The associates you'll be meeting haven't rehearsed for this, so you should get nothing but honest answers.

"Okay, let's go," said Jennifer. "Are you ready?"

We both answered in the affirmative and followed Jennifer out of the conference room and into her world of Operational Excellence.

Chapter 8

The Tour

As we walked through the hallways to the industrial claims processing area, I had an unexpected feeling of excitement, like a kid at a birthday party about to unwrap the big gift. Jennifer had presented a really good case for Operational Excellence. She explained the need for flow, how to create flow, and even discussed ways to identify broken flow and empower the team to repair it. It all made sense, and now I was looking forward to seeing it in action.

Just before we set foot in the office, Jennifer stopped us and said, "Let me give you a quick overview of what you'll see on the tour. Generally speaking, we're going to follow the flow from when a claim is initiated all the way through to the last step before it goes out to the customer.

"First, we're going to visit the area where flow begins for industrial claims processing. After that, we'll see a claims preparation cell, which prepares work for the claims processing cell, the last place we'll visit. Any questions? Alright, then let's get to it."

We made our way to the first area. When we arrived, I stood back and took it in. There were two rows of cubicles separated by a center hallway. The row on the left was marked by a sign that said "Information Reconciliation – All Claims" and the row on the right was identified by a sign that said "Industrial Claims Initialization Point." I saw what looked like a FIFO lane feeding the row of cubicles on the right. It seemed like these two areas were connected, but I wasn't sure exactly how, so I turned to Jennifer and asked, "Does the reconciliation area feed its work to the claims area through that FIFO rack?"

"I'm glad you can see that," she replied. "The reconciliation area handles all the incoming traffic for our industrial claims processing division as well as a substantial amount of volume for other areas, which means it's one of our major shared resources."

"Okay, but why don't the industrial claims people reconcile their own claims?" I asked.

"Good question," said Jennifer. "As I'm sure is the case with your business, Pat, when claims reach us, they're liable to be missing all sorts of information. To get that data, we may need to contact several people from different departments or even doctors, hospitals, patients, and others.

"So, instead of randomly chasing the missing information, we set up work-flow cycles and bring people together at preset times everyday to acquire it. Any requests for information or clarification take place right here, whether the source is internal or external. The associates reconcile claims while they're together, and then feed them to the appropriate areas through FIFO. Remember, we don't want to release claims with missing information into the flow because they'll disrupt it."

"So, you've essentially taken all the chaos that used to exist everywhere in the office and frontloaded it to this area," I said.

"In a way, yes," Jennifer replied. "We moved all of the variation that disrupted flow to the front where we can see it and address it. However, we also think of this area as one of the key points where we capture knowledge. Remember, in the office, we flow information and knowledge. Since we need to have certain knowledge to process the claim in flow, we make sure we have it before we release the claim. We can also use this knowledge as a reference point for future claims that present us with similar challenges. That way, we won't have to try to solve the same problem twice, or even more often, like we used to."

"That's pretty interesting," responded Peyton as I nodded in agreement.

"And what about the row of cubicles on the right? What happens when claims enter the FIFO rack?" I asked.

Jennifer pointed to the cubicles on her right and said, "Once a claim has all the information it needs, it gets placed into the FIFO lane that feeds this area. This is the actual initialization point for industrial claims, the exact point at which claims are released into the flow for industrial claims processing.

"When an associate finishes the claim he or she is working on, they simply withdraw the claim that's next in line in the FIFO lane. It's first come, first served. No shuffling priorities, no changing the sequence. Once the claim hits the FIFO lane, it remains in that sequence all the way to the customer."

"So, once a claim is pulled from the FIFO rack and released into the flow, there are no outstanding issues with it, right?" I asked.

"That's right, Pat," said Jennifer. "Since the associates in the cubicles on the right have all the information they need, they should be able to do their work without any issues. And, because of the work-flow cycles that govern this area, once a claim gets here, it's guaranteed to leave within three hours. From there, the flow continues and the rest of the work-flow cycles kick in. Because of those work-flow cycles, we know that at this point in the flow, each claim is precisely five days away from the customer. In fact, we're so confident in that timeframe, we even post it."

Jennifer pointed to a sign that was fixed to the side of one of the cubicles.

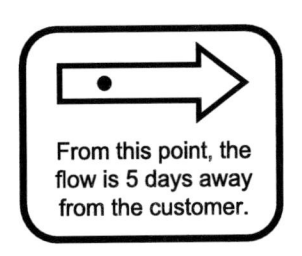

> From this point, the flow is 5 days away from the customer.

I had to admit, the sign was impressive. I gathered my thoughts about everything I'd seen and commented, "It sounds like the biggest pain point for this area is that incoming claims still don't have complete information. If you could move them through the information reconciliation area faster, you'd be able to get them out to the customer sooner."

"That's right," said Jennifer. "And that's one of the things we're going to address next. We'll be working with our customers to develop flow level standard work between us and them, which we expect will eliminate a lot of the chaos. Then, our next step is to teach our customers, doctors' offices, hospitals, etc., the techniques they need to create guaranteed turnaround times for responding to our inquiries. Once we get more experience under our belt, we'd love to teach them about Operational Excellence in its entirety. Any questions about the single point of initialization?"

"It all seems to make sense, but it's a lot to take in," I said.

Peyton nodded and Jennifer said, "Okay, let's continue on and follow the flow to the next area, which is our claims preparation cell. This cell combines information from the customer, account managers, and adjusters, and prepares it for the claims processing cell, which we will see next. Everyone at the claims preparation cell will be busy, but we can pull some people away briefly to answer any questions you might have."

We made our way back through the corridors and headed towards a group of four people arranged around a set of tables. Before we got there, Peyton noticed something on the wall and stopped. I saw it, too, and said to Jennifer, "That looks like what you drew on the flip chart back in the conference room."

I recognized the work-flow cycle symbol, and the information below it identified this group of people as the claims preparation cell. It also said they flowed work everyday for four hours, beginning at 1:00 p.m. And, I noticed a sign I had seen at our first stop, but with different information here.

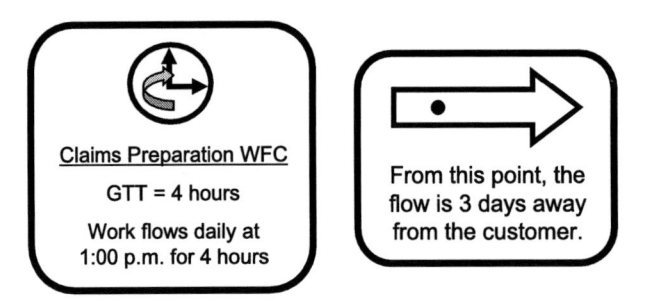

Claims Preparation WFC
GTT = 4 hours
Work flows daily at 1:00 p.m. for 4 hours

From this point, the flow is 3 days away from the customer.

"I'm surprised you recognize it, given my lack of artistic talent," Jennifer said, laughing.

"Wow," I said to Jennifer as Peyton listened in. "They're so confident in their work-flow cycles that they've posted their guaranteed turnaround times at every point in the flow."

"Well, it's true we post them," began Jennifer, "but it's not because of confidence. We want everyone to know not only how the information flows, but also the timing of the flow. Our goal is to make it so apparent that even a visitor can tell. So, what do you think? Are we successful?"

"Sure, I can follow it," answered Peyton. "It's quite easy. How about you, Pat?"

"Well, I've been in offices before that have lots of signs," I said. "But I've never seen visuals like this that describe the flow. They're very intuitive, and yes, I can follow them, too.

"But, I do have a question about one of them. I saw a sign at the initialization point that said the flow is five days away from the customer. But here, the same sign says the flow is three days away. Have I missed something?"

"Not at all, Pat," said Jennifer. "Don't forget that there are different types of work-flow cycles. Some are associated with the cells themselves and others pertain to the connections between the cells. Our initialization point connects to the claims preparation cell through a FIFO lane, and that connection has a work-flow cycle of one day. So, the work sits in the FIFO lane for one day before the claims preparation cell processes it. That's why the initialization point is five days away from the customer and the claims preparation cell is three, not four."

"I see," I said. "So, the time associated with a work-flow cycle could be the wait time in the FIFO lane plus the time in the next area where the work is processed?"

"That's right," replied Jennifer. "Remember, work-flow cycles refer to the rate at which work moves or flows within or between different areas or activities along a specific pathway, and they happen at preset times. A short pathway might be the processing area itself, while a long one might be the combination of two processing areas and the connection between them. It's up to you how big you make your work-flow cycles. We've tried to create ours so the associates in the work-flow cycle can see the end-to-end flow within that cycle."

"That makes sense," I replied. "It seems like that would help everyone see the flow of value, especially their part in it."

I focused my attention on the people in the claims preparation cell and asked Jennifer, "Can I ask some questions?"

"Ask away," said Jennifer. She introduced me to one of the associates, a woman named Wendy. She occupied the first position in the claims preparation cell.

After the introductions, I asked, "So, Wendy, how can you or anyone here know whether you're on time?"

"Well," responded Wendy, "we're able to monitor the flow throughout the day by that rack right there. It's color-coded green, yellow, and red to show us if things are going right or starting to go wrong. Green is good – everything is going okay. Yellow is a warning track, and if it's in the red, we have to do something. It's a pretty easy way to know if we're on time."

"Okay," I said. "But when will your boss or supervisor know if things are on time?"

"Every day at 5:00 p.m.," answered Wendy. "That's when we normally finish processing everything, and we use visual indicators to show that, too. At the end of the work-flow cycle for the claims preparation cell, we put a green flag on top of the tables here. About five minutes later, our supervisor comes around. If he sees the green flag, he knows everything got out on time today. It takes about thirty seconds out of his day. It's that quick. And there's an added benefit as well."

"What's that?" I asked.

"The boss hardly bothers us anymore, if you know what I mean," she said, laughing.

"But what if things haven't gotten out on time?" I pressed. "Don't you think he'd want to know before the end of the work-flow cycle?"

"True," said Wendy. "The boss can walk by anytime and see if work is backed up into the red zone. If it is, he might check in with us to see if we need any help. Once in a while we do, but not too often. Usually, we recognize we're drifting into red territory and we know how to take care of it ourselves. Even if he sees we're continuing to work past our work-flow cycle because of higher than normal customer demand, he knows we're taking care of it."

"Thanks," I said. "That clears things up for me."

"Anytime," responded Wendy.

I was beginning to see what Operational Excellence looked like. Their supervisor only spends about thirty seconds a day checking to see if things are on time? That's incredible! I was anxious to find out more.

I recalled the five questions for business process flow Jennifer introduced me to earlier in the day, and decided to test them out on one of the people working in the cell. If the questions really were as powerful and meaningful as Jennifer said, then anyone here should be able to answer them. Since Wendy happened to be right next to me, I decided to ask her.

"Wendy," I began, "do you mind if I bother you for a few more minutes?"

"Not at all, Pat," she replied. "What else can I do for you?"

"I just have some basic questions I was wondering if you could answer," I said.

"I'll do my best," she said. "Fire away."

"How do you know what to work on next?" I asked.

"That one's easy," said Wendy. "I do whatever is next in that rack right there." She pointed to it and said, "I just grab the next folder and get to it. It's first come, first served."

That also answered my next question: where do you get your work from? "Alright, and how long should it take you to perform your work?" I asked.

"Well, the claims are all a little different, depending on the type," said Wendy. "But each type has a standard time associated with it, and I can usually process the claim in that amount of time."

I was beginning to understand the power of these five questions. They took care of everything involved with normal flow and eliminated the need for management intervention. "Okay, last two questions," I said. "Where do you send your work once you're finished with it? And when do you send your completed work?"

"And here I was worried these questions were going to be difficult," said Wendy, smiling. "Jennifer already taught us the five questions for business process flow. Once I'm finished with my work, I send it to the next person, who happens to be the account manager in the claims preparation cell. We even mark the exact location with a big circle that says 'Next' on it. And I send it when that space opens up, and not a second before."

"Thanks again," I said. Wow, not only did Wendy know the answer to all five questions, she obviously understood their purpose. It was impressive to see how ingrained Operational Excellence is in the culture here.

Wendy said her goodbyes and Jennifer motioned over someone else from the processing cell so I could talk to him. He introduced himself as Steve and we distanced ourselves a little bit from the group. I asked him, "So, tell me the truth. Have the changes really made your life easier?"

"Oh, without a doubt," said Steve. "Everything's much more intuitive now, and we can all see how things are supposed to work. If there's a problem, everyone can see it. Before, we just heard about it afterwards from management. And if I have any questions, I simply ask my neighbor, who is always there when we prepare a claim. We don't have to chase people for information anymore, so there's a lot less disruption in my day. In fact, I probably deal with half the number of emails and voicemails I used to. And we haven't had any fiascoes with our customers in quite a while."

Fiascoes. Mercy Hospital, the catalyst for my visit here, flashed into my mind, and all at once my work problems came rushing back. "Steve, you said life is easier, but what about your customers? Do you think the changes have made them happy as well?" I asked.

"I think they might actually be happier than we are," Steve said with a smile. "With the guaranteed turnaround times, we now know how far away a claim is from the customer at every step in the flow. We don't have to guess anymore, we *know*. And the lead time has gotten significantly shorter for everyone."

"But what about when there are problems?" I asked. "How is this process any better than the way things used to be done?"

"Look, Pat, problems are going to happen no matter what system you have," said Steve. "We certainly have fewer problems now than in the past, but when they do occur, at least we're able to see them, react to them, and hopefully fix them before they impact the customer. And we don't need management standing over our shoulders all the time. That's quite a change from how things were before."

Jennifer came over and said we were ready to move to the last area. On the walk over, she reminded us we were going to see the claims processing cell. We arrived at a conference room, smaller than the one we had been in all morning. It had some tables, computers, and chairs, and between the computer terminals were circles with the word "Next" written in them. I could also see inbound and outbound FIFO lanes, and the inbound one seemed broken up into sections. And, I saw two signs I was very familiar with by now.

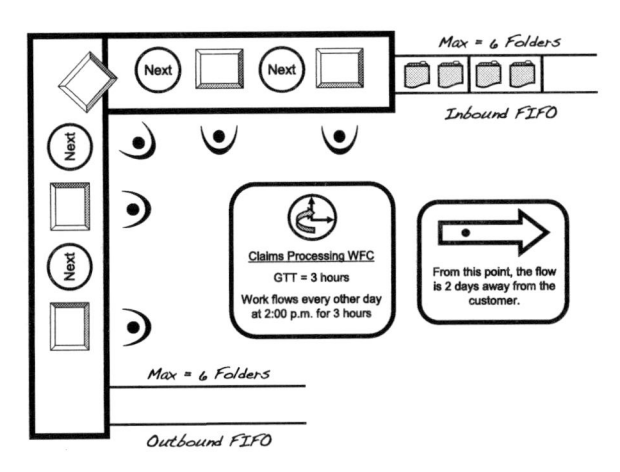

Max = 6 Folders

Inbound FIFO

Claims Processing WFC
GTT = 3 hours
Work flows every other day at 2:00 p.m. for 3 hours

From this point, the flow is 2 days away from the customer.

Max = 6 Folders

Outbound FIFO

Jennifer said, "This is the claims processing cell. Just like at our last cell, remember that we really have two levels of work-flow cycles here. One governs the claims processing cell itself, and the other governs the connection between this cell and the claims preparation cell. They're both important, because only together do they create a guaranteed turnaround time for the entire flow."

Right at 2:00 p.m., a group of five people came in, sat down, greeted each other, and began working. Jennifer walked us around to the different associates and introduced us. All of them said that if we had any questions, we should feel free to ask. Rather than jump right in, Jennifer suggested that Peyton and I stand back and watch them work for a little bit.

After observing for about ten minutes, I saw something remarkable happen. One of the associates in the flow took a folder off of the circle that said "Next" on it, opened it up, examined it for a few moments, and then sent it back to the previous associate. I motioned for Jennifer to step outside the conference room so I could ask her a question.

"Jennifer," I said. "What just happened there? I saw someone pick up a folder like they were going to start working on it, but instead they just returned it."

"Well, I can't say specifically what happened without going over and asking," said Jennifer. "But I'm pretty sure the previous associate in the flow did something wrong on the file, so it was sent back."

"Just like that?" I asked. "No one had to check or approve it?"

Jennifer looked slightly puzzled at my question, and then said, "No, why would they? Each associate knows what work they should receive, so if something is missing, they just send it back. That's one of the great things about flow. Before, the associate would put down the folder on his or her desk and, of course, stop the flow. Then, the voicemails and emails would begin."

I remembered what Steve had told me earlier about the number of his voicemails and emails being cut in half.

"In the processing cells," Jennifer continued, "the associates are able to see flow beginning to break down and take steps to fix it, *without a meeting and without management intervention.*"

I nodded to convey my understanding and we returned to the claims processing cell. Jennifer noted that everyone always knows what to work on next because they're working in flow that happens along a preset pathway. I asked Jennifer if I could ask one of the associates a question. She said it wasn't a problem so I went up to the first associate in the processing cell.

"Excuse me," I began as I pointed to the rack of folders that made up the FIFO lane. "I was wondering if you could tell me why your inbound FIFO lane is divided into sections."

"Sure thing," was the reply. "That's how we're able to tell what the customer demand is for the day. There are three sections to the FIFO lane and, depending on how many folders we have on a given day, we make adjustments as needed."

"Are there any meetings or managers involved in the decision?" I asked.

I got a look that suggested I should have known the answer already.

"We haven't done that in a while," the associate responded. "We just take care of it ourselves. We like it that way. Besides, my manager's got more important things to do with her time."

I went back to where Jennifer and Peyton were standing, then Jennifer led us out of the conference room, saying thank you to the associates as we left. Once outside, I had one more question.

"Jennifer, how has Operational Excellence affected your ability to hit your promise dates?" I asked.

Jennifer replied, "It's had an extremely positive impact. We've not only significantly reduced the overall claims processing time, but we're able to hit the new time consistently because we have work-flow cycles and guaranteed turnaround times at the cell and connection level everywhere in our flow. We know this because it's one of the things we measure. After all, in business, you are what you measure.

"Think of it this way, Pat. Imagine you were the supervisor or manager in charge of the claims processing cell we just saw. As a leader, if you knew that group flowed information for three hours every other day, would you need to chase after them to find out when their work would be finished?"

"Well, it'd be a bit of a mental adjustment to make, but I suppose not," I said. "If this is the way things worked all the time, then I wouldn't need to call people and ask them when they were going to flow their work."

"That's right," said Jennifer. "That's the power of having work-flow cycles and guaranteed turnaround times."

Okay, I thought, that makes sense. The work-flow cycles and guaranteed turnaround times are truly powerful, and I can see how they eliminate the need to constantly check in on people.

Jennifer turned to both of us and said, "Okay, there's one final question I have to ask you both, and it's one that tests how well we've done in this area. Take a quick look back inside the conference room."

We did as she asked and then came back outside. "Can you tell if our flow is on time right now just by looking?" she asked. "Are things normal, or is there a problem?"

Neither one of us was expecting this question. We took one more look at the processing cell. Peyton was first to respond. "Everything looks fine.

I don't see anything in the red zone, so it looks like they're on time."

"I agree," I added. "There's no work backed up in the FIFO lane. Everything is 'in the green,' so to speak."

"Great," responded Jennifer. "Just remember, the point isn't that everything is going well right now. The point is that you can *tell* if it is just by looking. No questions, no meetings, no status updates."

Jennifer paused for a few moments to let that sink in. "Are you ready to head back to the conference room and wrap up?" she asked.

Peyton and I both nodded and followed Jennifer back through the corridors. When we got to our conference room, we sat down. I had some questions about the tour, so I asked, "Jennifer, everything looked very impressive. And I'm not just talking about the flow, but the associates' attitudes as well. They were proud of the changes. In my office, well, people like doing things their own way. If you try to change anything it just leads to meeting after meeting. How did you get the associates to not only do things differently, but to *enjoy* doing things differently?"

Jennifer let out a deep breath and said, "Pat, that's an excellent point. The physical changes to the office are one thing, but changing people is something else entirely. I'll admit it was difficult. There's a whole other chapter in change management that we didn't talk about today.

"When we began implementing the new concepts, we encountered people who had been employed with the company for years, and they were very knowledgeable. Each person had their own method for getting things done. And I'm not just talking about the associates. I'm talking about their managers, too! At first, the managers didn't want people leaving their areas to join processing cells or work-flow cycles. They wanted them to be available to work on priorities.

"We had to educate everyone on the concepts of Operational Excellence and how we use it to grow our business. Creating awareness and aligning the managers was key. We had to teach everyone that it's not about increasing efficiency. It's about creating a foundation for business growth.

"It took a good deal of education as well as a strong dose of change management. Most people didn't see why we needed to create flow and establish standard work, but some did, and we worked with those people first. It was easier to persuade everyone else to give it a try once they saw it in action. We gave them some ownership in growing the business, too, and this helped put everyone at ease. After all, everyone wants to see the company grow."

"That makes sense," I said. "But it also sounds like quite a bit of work."

"It sure does," added Peyton. "But, then again, they did it here, and it's quite unlike anything I've ever seen. It's quite an accomplishment. You must be proud."

"We couldn't have done it without the associates," said Jennifer, smiling. "They're the real reason for our success. I give them all the credit."

We all agreed. Another question popped into my head and I said, "Jennifer, there's something else from the tour I want to ask you about. All the work was passed in folders. It was all hard copy. Everything could be held in your hand. But in many offices, the work is all electronic. In large companies, people send emails back and forth from different buildings and may never be in the same room. What do you do in situations like that?"

"That's a great question, Pat," said Jennifer. "We still want to follow the same process and use the same techniques we've been talking about. However, the application will be a little different. Let's just say there are many ways to create end-to-end flow by following the guidelines. The only limit to your specific situation is your creativity. If you can find a way to answer the five questions for flow, you should be okay.

"For example, we can create rules for our email inboxes so messages are sent into electronic FIFO lanes. From there, we'd process them the same way we process work in the FIFO racks you saw on the tour. Offsite locations would establish their work-flow cycles so they flow information to us when we need it."

I nodded and Peyton said, "With a little creativity, I can see how the guidelines would simplify the flow between different branches all over the country."

"And that's exactly what they've done for us," said Jennifer. She paused before continuing. "Okay, great discussion. Your questions have reminded me just how much we've accomplished. Before we conclude, I want to thank both of you for taking time out of your day to come here and visit with us. I hope you learned a lot of practical knowledge so far, but we've got one more critical topic to cover, so I'd like to wrap up with a final thought. I'd like for you to think of what it is you *didn't* see while we were out on the tour."

Peyton and I both looked at each other for a second, then thought about it. What didn't we see? There could be a million different answers to that question, but I sensed Jennifer was after something very specific. I thought back to the conversation we'd just had about work-flow cycles and guaranteed turnaround times, and how Peyton and I knew the claims processing cell was on time just by looking. Then, it hit me.

"Managers," I said, delighted. "We didn't see any managers or supervisors on the tour. No one was walking around checking on things or putting out fires. We also didn't see any hot list, expedites, or changing priorities. There weren't any meetings taking place in any of the open rooms either. Does management even have meetings to set priorities anymore?"

"Not really," replied Jennifer. "We had a few when we first implemented the system, but we've virtually eliminated them. Which leads me to my final point of the day. Are your ready?"

"Remember one of the things we said earlier about Operational Excellence? It's a foundation for business growth. Our objective is to grow the business. This is why Operational Excellence is the destination of the continuous improvement journey. A seamless, smooth-running operation *enables managers to spend their time working on offense!"*

Offense? I thought. Are we talking about football?

"Working on offense means performing activities that grow the business as opposed to maintaining or defending it," said Jennifer. "Think about it. If you're out there chasing claims, people, and resources all day, how will you ever have the time you need to grow your business? To grow your business, you need *time*. And our managers and supervisors now *have time to work on offense*, or growing our business.

"This is why we work so hard following and implementing the business process guidelines for flow. We do it for one reason: to give our people the time they need to work on offense."

It all made sense to me now. The business process guidelines for flow were enough of a paradigm shift. To find out they were also a means to an even greater end – that was incredible. For years, I'd just been trying to improve my office for efficiency and productivity, when I really should have been trying to improve it to *grow the business.*

I stood up to leave and went over and shook Jennifer's hand, then Peyton's. "Thanks for everything," I said to her. "Now, I've got to go back and convince my boss that I haven't been dreaming all day."

Jennifer chuckled a little before saying, "Don't worry, Pat. It won't be as hard as it seems. Just remember everything we talked about today, especially how Operational Excellence creates a foundation for business growth and frees up management to work on offense. If your boss is anything like mine, that'll get eaten right up."

I thanked my companions once again and made my way out of the building and to my car. On the drive home and later that night, I couldn't stop thinking about what I had learned and seen. How could I possibly explain it all to Chris tomorrow?

Chapter 9

Sharing the Knowledge

When the alarm sounded on Friday, I bolted out of bed, anxious to get to the office to meet with Chris. What a week! Only four mornings ago, I learned about the mess that happened while I was away. But what I've seen and heard since has changed the way I look at the office. I was aware of the tough sell ahead and the skepticism I expected to encounter, but I was ready for the challenge.

I got into my car and headed to work, rehearsing the pending encounter with Chris along the way. I parked and, as I walked to the office, noticed Chris looking at me from the window on the third floor, as if awaiting my arrival. At that moment, I was glad I had prepared for this discussion.

The ride up the elevator seemed to take forever. As the doors opened, Chris met me, seemingly eager to hear about my field trip yesterday. We walked straight into my office. I didn't have a chance to check email or voicemail.

"So, I'm really interested in what you learned from the benchmarking trip yesterday," said Chris. "Mercy Hospital called again and wants an update on how we are going to correct things. It sure would be good to have a plan to share with them before this escalates."

I took a deep breath and gathered my thoughts. "Okay," I said, "as we're both well aware, we discovered a downward trend in our performance that we need to correct or we risk alienating or losing Mercy Hospital and other major customers. And, since some of our smaller customers have tremendous potential for growth, any plan we put in place has to take care of all of our customers, not just the ones who are most important right now. I won't bother going into any more detail on these issues since you're as familiar with them as I am."

"Possibly more familiar," said Chris, "but who's keeping score, right?"

"Right," I said. Well, no point in wasting any time, I thought. "Let me get right into what I saw and heard yesterday, what my approach was when I first got there, and what I'd like to share with you today.

"For starters, I admit that I was hoping I'd be able to simply copy what they did there and paste it here to solve our problems. We've been using some continuous improvement tools ever since I got here, so I figured if this other company was using them better or more effectively, I'd just see how and try to do the same thing here.

"But they looked at continuous improvement differently. They had moved beyond solving problems, eliminating waste, and simply trying to get better each day. They looked at creating Operational Excellence. They set a destination for what they were trying to accomplish with their continuous improvement efforts. And, since they knew where they were going, they were able to get there much faster than they otherwise would have."

"That's interesting," said Chris. "You mentioned Operational Excellence. Every company says that's what they're striving for, even us. Aren't we doing that already?"

"Not exactly," I said. "We're just trying to continuously improve by using the latest tools, but they're trying to get to a place where *'Each and every employee can see the flow of value to the customer, and fix that flow before it breaks down.'* That's how they define Operational Excellence, by the way, and it's by far the most practical and applicable definition I've ever heard."

"Hmmm..." said Chris, letting that sink in. "That's quite a definition, and when I think about it, that's pretty much exactly what I want to see happening here. I like it. Keep going."

"Well, I went there looking to solve our problems, but now, I'm seeing things from a much broader perspective," I said. "It's not about looking for solutions to problems. It's about *growing our business.*"

"Growing our business?" repeated Chris. "I'm starting to like this even more."

"It was quite an insight," I said. "We strive for Operational Excellence not only to create 'self-healing' flow, but to grow our business."

"Sounds good," said Chris. "But how do we do that when we're still having problems with some of our key customers?"

"This is the real beauty of it," I said. "We're going to do it by *following a process*. One of the first things I learned yesterday was that we can't just copy their solution and paste it here. But we can copy the *process* they used."

"Okay, that makes sense," said Chris. "Our business is different from theirs anyway."

"And even better," I replied, "*a process can be taught*, and it can be shared with everyone in the company and used again and again to generate results. This is how they changed over there, and it's how we can change here, too."

"It must be some process," said Chris, with a little bit of disbelief. "But I like what you said about how we're able to teach it to everyone. That's a good thought. Tell me more."

I felt like I was getting somewhere. "Sure thing," I said. "One of the first things I learned was that we want to create flow through our office. To determine if we have flow, we need to ask five questions, and if we can answer them all successfully, we have flow. I won't get into the details of those questions now, but suffice it to say that everything is so systematic that even something as seemingly simple as creating flow is done by following a process."

"Okay," said Chris, "so there's a process for creating flow. And that's supposed to transform this office into something spectacular?"

"Sort of," I answered, "but not by itself. The five questions I just mentioned are used to determine whether we have flow. There's actually an eight-step process to create flow through the entire office, one that we can teach and everyone can learn. It includes things like processing cells, work-flow cycles, standard work at the activity, flow, and improvement level, and visual indicators that tell us whether or not we're on time. And, get this: if we have flow through our entire office, then we can establish a guaranteed turnaround time for every single claim we get.

"You see, Chris, I learned that we should flow information along predetermined, physical pathways at preset times and in first-in, first-out (FIFO) fashion. Everyone knows the pathways and timing involved, so they know when they'll get the information they need. No one has to make any phone calls or chase people or information. Once that flow is established, we get everyone to see it with visual indicators, which the associates use to distinguish normal flow from abnormal flow. The result is that the flow 'self-heals' when things start to go wrong. The associates fix the flow before it breaks down, and they do so *without management intervention*."

"Pat, this is a breakthrough. It's quite a different way of thinking, and it sounds like just what we need," said Chris. "But, you talked about growing our business. How is this process going to do that?"

"By freeing up management to work on *offense*," I said, surprised at how fluidly that rolled off my tongue. "And by offense, I mean growing the business. We use an eight-step process to create flow through our entire office but, again, the secret is that the associates handle it all by themselves. They're able to see when it's about to break down and fix it on their own.

"Once the system is in place, there's practically no management intervention whatsoever. And since managers aren't spending their time chasing claims, people, and resources, they finally have the time they need to grow the business."

Chris leaned back and let out a deep breath before speaking. "You know, I've been trying to figure out how to explain that to people for a long time now. I'm getting pressure from the top to spend more of my time generating new business, but I don't have the time because I'm here ten hours a day just making sure everything gets done.

"I like it, Pat. I have to tell you, you've killed two *big* birds with one stone. Putting in self-healing flow that creates guaranteed turnaround times *and* frees up management to work on offense? I can see our market share growing already. So, I have two questions for you. How long and how much?"

"That's what's so great about Operational Excellence," I said. "It takes months, not years, because everyone works toward a common destination and follows a process to get there. As for the cost, it's all education, and whatever expense we incur will no doubt be offset by the business we'll gain and fiascoes we'll avoid. No more Mercy Hospital breathing down our necks, no more shuffling priorities, no more wondering when a claim will be completed."

"So you, we, our company, can do all of this right now?" asked Chris.

"Well, I understand the concepts, and think I can give them a shot," I said. "But after what I saw yesterday, I know there's a lot more to learn. The first thing we need to do is get the executives aligned and onboard. That's one of the most important steps. Without understanding at the top of the organization, everything else becomes a lot more complicated. Then, like I said before, we use education to get everyone – executives, managers, and associates – moving toward a common destination of Operational Excellence."

I paused to catch my breath. I eyed Chris for a few moments, looking for a reaction, and then said, "So, what do you think?"

Chris stood up, went to the door, and said, "I think I need to get educated. Put me first on the list. And Pat…good job."

THE END
(and the beginning)

The Institute for Operational Excellence

The Institute for Operational Excellence is an advanced educational center founded to teach companies how to achieve Operational Excellence. Located in North Kingstown, RI, the Institute for Operational Excellence defines Operational Excellence in a way that all employees, from top executives to front line associates, can understand and apply to their respective environments.

The Institute for Operational Excellence teaches university-style public classes using case studies, textbooks, and hands-on simulations. It also hosts public, private, and supply chain conferences for companies looking to accelerate their efforts to achieve Operational Excellence in all areas of business. The Institute's book series teaches readers how to achieve Operational Excellence in different areas of the organization, and its products are designed to streamline continuous improvement and help companies build momentum quickly to achieve Operational Excellence.

To learn more, or to join the Institute's complimentary membership, contact The Institute for Operational Excellence.

    Phone: 401-667-0117
    Web: www.instituteopex.org
    Email: info@instituteopex.org

Duggan Associates

While The Institute for Operational Excellence focuses on providing public education to increase awareness about Operational Excellence, Duggan Associates is an authorized service provider that specializes in customized, onsite training using a company's unique products and processes. Duggan Associates works hand-in-hand with companies to teach them how to apply the principles of Operational Excellence in their organization. They specialize in the practical, guided, and immediate application of knowledge to help companies achieve Operational Excellence quickly.

To learn more, contact Duggan Associates.

Phone: 401-667-7299
Web: www.dugganinc.com
Email: info@dugganinc.com

En Español: www.dugganinc.mx

Feedback

Comments? Visit the 'Books & Products' page on www.instituteopex.org and tell the authors what you think.

Further Reading List

Duggan, Kevin J. <u>Creating Mixed Model Value Streams: Practical Lean Techniques for Building to Demand.</u> Productivity Press, 2002.

Keyte, Beau and Drew Locher. <u>The Complete Lean Enterprise: Value Stream Mapping for Administrative and Office Processes.</u> Productivity Press, 2004.

Liker, Jeffery K. <u>The Toyota Way: 14 Management Principles from The World's Greatest Manufacturer.</u> McGraw-Hill, 2004.

Rother, Mike and John Shook. <u>Learning To See: Value-Stream Mapping to Create Value and Eliminate Muda.</u> The Lean Enterprise Institute, 2003.

Womack, James P. and Daniel T. Jones. <u>Lean Thinking: Banish Waste and Create Wealth in Your Corporation.</u> Simon & Schuster, 1996.